Integrating the ESL Standards Into Classroom Practice:
Grades Pre-K–2

Betty Ansin Smallwood, Editor

WRITERS

Carla Frye

Judie Haynes

Sonia James

Carrie Martin

Judith B. O'Loughlin

Esther Retish

Betty Ansin Smallwood

Suzanne Irujo, Series Editor

TESOL™ Teachers of English to Speakers of Other Languages, Inc.

Typeset in Optima with Dolphin Display
by Capitol Communications Systems, Inc., Crofton, Maryland USA
and printed by Pantagraph Printing, Bloomington, Illinois USA

Teachers of English to Speakers of Other Languages, Inc.
700 South Washington Street, Suite 200
Alexandria, Virginia 22314-4287 USA
Tel. 703-836-0774 • Fax 703-836-7864 • E-mail tesol@tesol.org • http://www.tesol.org/

Director of Communications and Marketing: Helen Kornblum
Managing Editor: Marilyn Kupetz
Copy Editor: Marcia R. Annis
Additional Reader: Ellen Garshick
Cover Design: Charles Akins and Ann Kammerer

ISBN 0-939791-84-6
Library of Congress Catalogue No. 00-130571

Contents

Acknowledgments

Yemi thanked the mat vendor and other trades people for taking care of her younger brother Kokou, who had wandered away from her during market day in their West African village. "She said, 'Thank you,' again and again and again . . . ." (Cowen-Fletcher, 1994, p. 28). When she finally found her mother, who was selling mangoes, Mom was not worried about her children. She said, "You weren't alone today, Yemi. We don't raise our children by ourselves. 'It takes a village to raise a child.'" (p. 32).

And it takes a community to write a book. I want to take this opportunity to thank the various community members whose loving support helped breathe life into this book, our collective child. (I also would like to thank Jane Cowen-Fletcher, a former Peace Corps volunteer in Benin, West Africa, who blended this now famous African proverb into a beautiful children's book long before the phrase "it takes a village" became popular.)

Thank you first to the writers and their students. Thank you, Carla, Carrie, Esther, Judie, Judy, Shawn, and Sonia. We became a virtual community, sharing drafts and words of encouragement across the country via phone lines and cyberspace. To borrow the words of Carla Frye, "Big thanks to all the ESOL teachers for everything they have done for me and all students. I couldn't have survived without their love and support."

Thank you, Suzanne Irujo, for being a wonderful series editor. You have a gift for improving a piece of writing while maintaining the author's voice and intent, and you do this with care, respect, and attention to detail. The quality of your work and your character are invisibly reflected throughout our volume. It has been a privilege to work with you.

Thank you to the other volume editors: Barbara Agor, Suzanne Irujo, and Katharine Davies Samway. I was especially appreciative of our professional dialogues at the beginning of the process, as we engaged in often passionate exchanges about the overall goals of the series and then translated these into concrete guidelines that would work across all four volumes.

Thank you, Marilyn Kupetz, for being so knowledgeable in your position as managing editor at TESOL. It was comforting to know you had the answers to our many questions about manuscript details, artwork, and copyrights, and that you would always answer promptly. Thank you also to Marcia Annis, copy editor; I appreciated your careful readings and attention to details. I enjoyed working with both of you, and knew our volume was in good hands.

Thank you, Kathleen Graves, in your capacity as chair of the TESOL Publications Committee, for introducing me to the project and inviting me onto this editorial team.

Last, but not least, thanks to my family members, Jonah and John. My home office is across the hall from my teenage son Jonah's room. We used to do a lot of cooperative play. Now we seem to do more parallel work. If I glance left from my computer, I can check on him working (or playing) on his computer. We often talk across the hallway in the evenings, sharing ideas, asking questions, and just chatting. Thank you, Jonah, for being my work partner, and my distraction partner, during this book project, and for being such a great kid.

My husband, John, has been my best friend for over 30 years now. I cannot thank him enough for all his encouragement and for the hours he has patiently listened to me and to my thousands of questions. He also shoulders my share of household and family responsibilities, when my work and deadlines take priority. I try to do the same for him. I cannot imagine this or any of my other projects being as successful without his ongoing, loving support. Thank you, John.

Thanks again to all our community members who have generously shared their gifts to give life to this volume, which we now humbly share with you.

REFERENCE

Cowen-Fletcher, J. (1994). *It takes a village*. New York: Scholastic.

Series Editor's Preface

When I first saw a copy of *ESL Standards for Pre-K–12 Students* (TESOL, 1997), I thought, "These are very well done, but how are teachers going to use them?" Working with teachers since then, I've heard them echo those thoughts: "I really like these standards, but I'm not sure how to use them in my classroom."

The four volumes in the series *Integrating the ESL Standards Into Classroom Practice* are designed to help teachers use the standards. The series covers four sets of grade levels: pre-K–2, 3–5, 6–8, and 9–12. Each volume contains six units, some designed with a particular grade level or proficiency level in mind, others designed to span grade and proficiency levels. There are units for very specific contexts and units that are more general. All the units are adaptable for other levels and contexts and include suggestions for doing that.

These units were taught and written by real teachers, each of whom approaches the implementation of the ESL standards in the classroom in a different way. As I worked on editing the four volumes, I was struck by the wide variety of ways in which teachers who work with standards use them to inform their teaching. In describing what skills must be mastered by ESOL students in public schools, the standards become planning tools, observational aids, assessment guides, and ways of understanding language development.

These units also exemplify the strategies that Lachat (1999) recommends for teachers implementing standards-based instruction:

- Organize learning around what students need to know and be able to do
- Enrich their teaching by cultivating students' higher order thinking processes
- Guide student inquiry by posing real-life tasks that require reasoning and problem-solving
- Emphasize holistic concepts rather than fragmented units of information
- Provide a variety of opportunities for students to explore and confront concepts and situations over time
- Use multiple sources of information rather than a single text
- Work in interdisciplinary teams
- Use multiple forms of assessment to gather concrete evidence of student proficiencies (p. 13)

The teachers who prepared these units did so to demonstrate what they did when they taught the units, not to tell others what should be done. The units were designed to serve several purposes. We wanted them to be complete, finished products, usable as they are in other classrooms, so we made them as explicit as we could. We wanted them to be adaptable for use in other situations and contexts, so we included suggestions for doing that. We wanted them to serve as possible models for teachers who want to develop their own standards-based units, so we provided explanations for why we did things as we did.

These volumes expand upon and complement the work contained in previous TESOL standards publications. We have used appropriate descriptors and sample progress indicators as they appear for each standard in *ESL Standards for Pre-K–12 Students* (TESOL, 1997), although we have also created some new progress indicators when appropriate. We have tried to incorporate the assessment process outlined in *Managing the Assessment Process: A Framework for Measuring Student Attainment of the ESL Standards* (TESOL, 1998). Many of the checklists and rubrics used in the assessment sections are adaptations of those found in *Scenarios for ESL Standards-Based Assessment* (TESOL, in press).

A few technical notes:

- In keeping with the terminology used in *ESL Standards* (TESOL, 1997), we use *ESL* (English as a second language) to refer to the standards, the field, and our classes. We use *ESOL* (English to speakers of other languages) to refer to the learners themselves.

- In order to avoid having to repeat detailed procedures for teaching techniques that appear in several units in a volume, we have included a glossary of techniques. Because of this, there is no glossary of terms, but definitions of standards-related terms are available in *ESL Standards* (TESOL, 1997) and *Scenarios* (TESOL, in press).

- All resources and references for each unit are listed at the end of the unit. Writers annotated the resources where they felt it would be helpful to readers.

Our hope in producing these volumes is that teachers will be able to use these units in their own classes and that they will also gain insights into incorporating the ESL standards into other units they may develop. We want them to be able to say, after reading one or several units, "Now I know what to do with the ESL standards in my classroom."

Suzanne Irujo, Series Editor

REFERENCES

Lachat, M. A. (1999). *Standards, equity and cultural diversity.* Providence, RI: Northeast and Islands Regional Educational Laboratory at Brown University (LAB).

TESOL. (1997). *ESL standards for pre-K–12 students.* Alexandria, VA: Author.

TESOL. (1998). *Managing the assessment process: A framework for measuring student attainment of the ESL standards* (TESOL Professional Paper No. 5). Alexandria, VA: Author.

TESOL. (in press). *Scenarios for ESL standards-based assessment.* Alexandria, VA: Author.

Introduction

In memory of Shel Silverstein, I use the words from one of his poems to invite you into this pre-K–2 volume of *Integrating the ESL Standards Into Classroom Practice*: "If you are a dreamer, a wisher, . . . a magic bean buyer, . . . come sit by my fire, for we have some flax-golden tales to spin. Come in!" (Silverstein, 1974, p. 9).

I am proud and excited to share this volume with you. It has been a labor of love for all of us, our small community of six primary school ESL teacher-writers. And frankly, it has been a challenge, too. Our mission was to integrate *ESL Standards for Pre-K–12 Students* (TESOL, 1997) into our local classroom practices through authentic thematic units and to do it in a consistent manner, using shared guidelines. The guidelines have caused us to adjust our individual styles, but they also helped bring unity to the volume and the series as a whole.

What I hope and believe you will find in this volume are fully developed, age- and ESL-appropriate thematic units rich with tried-and-true strategies, but infused with something new: the ESL standards. The ultimate test of the standards is to be able to bring them alive in our teaching and to make a difference for our students. This is what we have tried to do—to blend the best of the old and the new and to be open to change.

Please especially read what I call the *standards story* in each chapter. These stories provide powerful testimony to our individual journeys with the ESL standards. Some of our writers are further along in this journey, already using state and district standards along with the national ESL standards. Others are just beginning the journey. Nonetheless, we are all learning and invite you to do the same. Collectively, our stories indicate that using the ESL standards improves our planning, instruction, and assessment. They also provide a vehicle for professional dialogue among ESL and other educators and present our field as serious and substantive.

As editor, I have tried to create a sense of community among our team of writers. We are richly diverse, and I sought that diversity in building our community. We come from different backgrounds, live in different places, bring a range of experiences, work in different program types, teach different grades (within pre-K–2), have different styles, and chose to write about different topics. Yet for communities to be successful, they have to share common values, and we do. We are all committed to serving our English language learners; to working hard to write the best material for them; and to communicating and helping one another, on-line, on the phone, and in person. This is a fine community that reaches from California to New Jersey, from 20-year veterans to novice teachers, from BAs to those currently pursuing MAs to recent PhDs, and from a grandmother to a new mother.

As the editor, as well as a writer, I have often felt like the little red hen in the nursery tale (Galdone, 1973/1987), busily going through all the steps to produce bread. But when I asked for help or made requests along the way, my community members have not replied, "No, not I," but rather, "Yes, I will." That positive, can-do attitude pervades the individual units and also the collective spirit of our book community.

Let me take this opportunity to briefly introduce you to our community members, the six teacher-writers, and their stories, in the order in which they appear in the book.

Carla Frye teaches pre-K and early childhood ESOL learners in Newport News, Virginia. Her unit, "All About Me: Marvelous, Magnificent Me!" centers on children and their basic needs, including the family, then expands to school topics, and gradually introduces age-appropriate academic content and language. Carla's program model is a regular pre-K classroom consisting of more than 50% limited English speaking children, with herself as the lead teacher. In reality, Carla teaches in a variety of ESL program models, including ESL pullout and push-in models. The full classroom setting is her preferred model.

Sonia James teaches ESL and works as a program consultant in Bowling Green, Kentucky, where the ESL population has more than doubled in the past 3 years. Her unit, "Making Bread Together," adds a multicultural perspective to the breads and cereal food group, her science curriculum topic. Like Carla, Sonia works with young ESOL learners in a variety of ESL program models, but chose to highlight the inclusion model here. Sonia team-taught this unit with the kindergarten teacher in her school.

Esther Retish has taught ESL in Iowa City, Iowa, for many years. In "The World of Work: Choices and Opportunities," she presents a practical approach to a pragmatic topic. As a veteran ESL teacher, Esther naturally integrates the four skills of listening, speaking, reading, and writing with language, literature, and content, while building the home-school connection that is so important for young children. Esther taught this unit to her mixed-beginner ESL pullout class of first and second graders and also created an adapted version of this model for her ESL kindergarten group. She addresses both ages of English language learners in her chapter.

Judie Haynes and Judith B. O'Loughlin teach ESL in neighboring communities in northern New Jersey, River Edge and Ho-Ho-Kus School Districts, respectively. Both districts have fairly small, low-incidence ESL populations, which is a common phenomenon in many areas. This creates numerous challenges for the ESL teacher, including multiage and multilevel ESL classes. Judie and Judy have pooled their many talents to create this rich "'Eggs'citing Animals" unit that addresses these issues for a Grade 1–2 pullout ESL class. This content-based unit teaches the children everything from songs to science experiments, with plenty of reading and writing activities sandwiched in between.

Carrie Martin teaches second grade in the Ontario/Montclair School District of southern California. She uses her cross-cultural, language, and academic development (CLAD) training daily with her 90% Hispanic population, whose English proficiency ranges from beginning to fluent. Her social studies unit, "Exploring Native American Cultures: The Iroquois," is carefully designed to meet the California state standards and her district's standards as well as the national ESL standards. Carrie creatively blends cooperative groups and experiential learning with more traditional teaching to introduce a cultural group that is new to her students.

I taught ESL for 18 years as a classroom teacher, with 10 of those years in Montgomery County Public Schools, Maryland. My unit, "Our Global Community: Different but Alike," came from that experience and was developed as part of my doctoral dissertation research. I report on Shawn Martin's pilot teaching of this unit to her own regular second-grade classroom in Fairfax County Public Schools, Virginia. In Shawn's setting, there is a large multicultural population, with the intermediate-level ESOL students included (or pushed in) for the language arts block, where this unit was taught. I also compare how this unit was implemented in another program model—a pullout, beginning-level ESL class.

Writing and editing this volume has been a powerful professional development experience for all of us. My hope is that reading it will contribute to your own growth as an educator of young ESOL children. I think we all feel like the little blue engine in Piper's (1954/1985) classic children's story, who said "I think I can, I think I can, I think I can" (n.p.). We did it! We hope you enjoy our stories, learn from them, and believe that you can do it too. You absolutely can.

Betty Ansin Smallwood, Editor

REFERENCES

Galdone, P. (1973/1987). *The little red hen.* Boston: Houghton Mifflin.

Piper, W. (1954/1985). *The little engine that could.* New York: Platt & Munk.

Silverstein, S. (1974). The invitation. In *Where the sidewalk ends* (p. 9). New York: HarperCollins.

TESOL. (1997). *ESL standards for pre-K–12 students.* Alexandria, VA: Author.

UNIT 1
All About Me: Marvelous, Magnificent Me!

CARLA FRYE

Introduction

Children who start to learn a foreign language early in life can better understand their native language as they become conscious of the existence of language as a phenomenon. Their cultural outlook is wider than that of monolingual children who often believe that their own culture, their language and their customs are the only ones that matter in the world. The introduction of a foreign idiom into the child's world helps him to develop tolerance toward people different from him and in the long run contributes toward international understanding. (Titone, 1990, p. 10)

The pre-K students in Classroom 1 are getting ready for their literacy lesson. They are sitting quietly on the rug in front of the teacher as she

---

Context

Grade level: Pre-K

English proficiency levels: Mixed, including native speakers, native speakers with language disabilities, limited-English speakers, and non-English speakers

Native languages of students: English, Spanish, Kurdish, Chinese, Vietnamese

Focus of instruction: Socialization skills, basic vocabulary for academia, acculturation

Type of class: Mainstream, self-contained, pre-K class (half day), with a majority of ESOL children

Length of unit: 4 weeks

prepares to ask questions about the story. The students are fully engaged in the activity and ready for discussion:

Ms. Frye:	*Now, who can tell me what the title of our story is? Remember, before you raise your hand, I want you to tell me in a complete sentence.*
Angela:	*The title of our story is* The Lion and the Mouse.
Ms. Frye:	*Very good, Angela! Now, who can tell me the name of the author, the person who wrote the story?*
Luis:	*Avelyn Davidson.*
Ms. Frye:	*That is the correct answer Luis, but can you tell me that answer using a sentence?*
Luis:	*Uh . . . I dunno. Author Avelyn Davidson?*

I continue to work with Luis on sentence usage. Other students are continuously raising their hands and yelling out, anxious to answer with the appropriate response. I encourage full sentences to help develop my students' correct use of language. However, I accept phrases and less than sentences, especially when the information is correct, while trying to move the students along to fuller expression, based on their individual levels of proficiency. Eventually, Luis does answer the question with a complete sentence.

This reenactment is a typical classroom scenario that I go through daily with my 4-year-old ESOL students. It is very difficult for them to speak in complete sentences because many of them are non-English-speaking when they first enter my classroom. They are very curious and always want to do what they can to please their teachers.

My class is a mainstream pre-K classroom, but 13 of my 25 children are ESOL students. The others are African American (4) and Caucasian (8). Two are special needs students who participate in my classroom, with special education support, in an inclusion model. We follow the Title I First Step Curriculum Guide (Newport News Public Schools Revision Committee, 1994). I teach in the Newport News, Virginia, public schools. I am the mainstream classroom teacher, trained in ESL and early childhood education. In this pre-K class, there is also a special education pre-K teacher and a teacher's assistant.

Although I have also worked as a pullout ESL teacher, I prefer this whole-class model. It allows me to spend more time with my children, which makes a big impact on their knowledge, self-esteem, and eagerness to learn the language.

There is not a lot of information available regarding teaching pre-K ESOL children, and even less about using *ESL Standards for Pre-K–12 Students* (TESOL, 1997) with this age group. I hope the information in this unit will contribute to this knowledge base and also provide teachers with some creative ideas to use in their classrooms.

Unit Overview

The activities in this unit relate to basic curriculum goals required at the pre-K as well as the kindergarten level. Many of these activities can also be used with older primary and elementary grades by adapting them to make them age appropriate.

I teach this unit at the beginning of the year. My class is generally the first school experience for my students, and I want to make it a warm and welcoming one. Many of the lessons are very personal in the beginning. This helps us get to know one another and establish our friendships. I developed this unit because I wanted my ESOL students

Unit Overview: "All About Me"

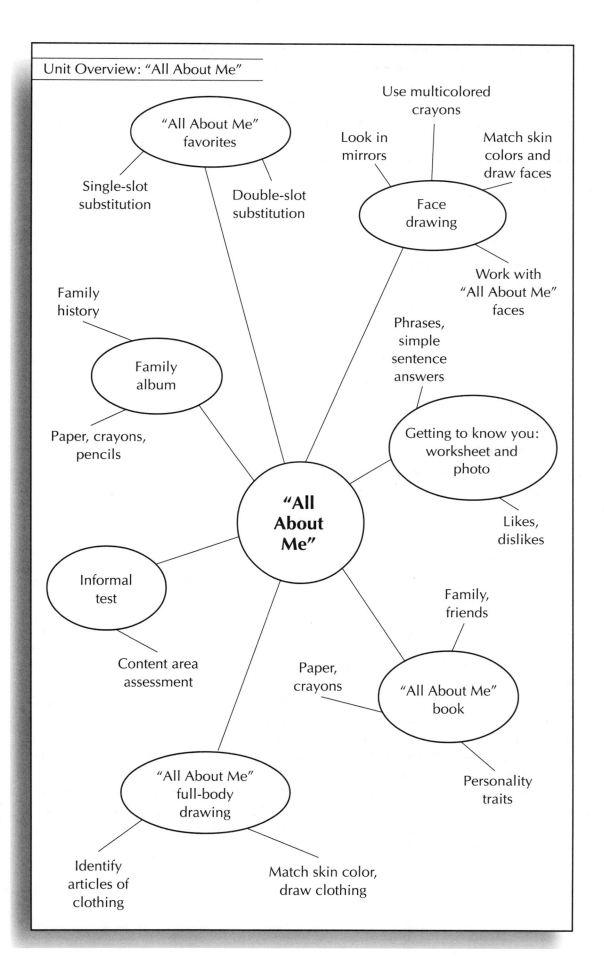

"All About Me" favorites

Single-slot substitution

Double-slot substitution

Use multicolored crayons

Look in mirrors

Match skin colors and draw faces

Face drawing

Work with "All About Me" faces

Family history

Family album

Paper, crayons, pencils

Phrases, simple sentence answers

"All About Me"

Getting to know you: worksheet and photo

Likes, dislikes

Informal test

Content area assessment

Family, friends

Paper, crayons

"All About Me" book

Personality traits

"All About Me" full-body drawing

Identify articles of clothing

Match skin color, draw clothing

to feel more confident about entering school for the first time and finding themselves in a new environment. It is a dramatic change for children to come to the United States. However, with this unit in place, I hope this change will be a smooth one.

This unit extends the concept of self to incorporate other curriculum areas, such as colors, numbers, shapes, and letters. These are some of the basic concepts that these children need to be familiar with before they enter kindergarten. These concepts are particularly important for children who are learning them for the first time, while they are learning English.

My goals for the unit are that students will

Content

- develop an awareness of colors
- develop an awareness of numbers
- develop an awareness of shapes
- develop an awareness of body parts and clothing

Language

- indicate comprehension of spoken English
- speak using complete sentences whenever possible
- develop an awareness of letters
- write letters on paper

Learning Strategies

- track what they are reading on paper
- develop observational skills
- interact with other people to develop a better awareness of self, family, and environment

The unit overview on page 3 shows the activities that make up the unit.

Standards

The ESL standards have been incorporated very smoothly into all the activities for this unit. Many times several of the standards can be linked with each activity. Working with pre-K children, I find that every standard seems to apply to one point or another during a lesson.

As I was planning this unit, I regularly referred to the standards. They provide unity to the varied techniques and activities that I do with my students. Using the standards, I feel that I share a common purpose with other ESL teachers, as we work in our different schools to help educate the ESOL children entrusted to our care. They also support the evaluation of the students as well as of the teacher.

I thoroughly believe that these standards are designed with our children in mind. Although most pre-K teachers already have a written curriculum that they follow, the standards add depth to it and make it more substantive for the children and the classroom environment. They have helped me a great deal with all my ESL and regular pre-K students, and I use them every day as part of my instruction.

Activities

Matching Skin Colors and Drawing Faces

PURPOSE: TO SHARE STUDENT-TO-STUDENT COMMUNICATION ABOUT SIMILAR FACIAL FEATURES AND SKIN TONES.

Goal 1, Standard 3 **To use English to communicate in social settings: Students will use learning strategies to extend their communicative competence.**

Descriptors

- listening to and imitating how others use English
- focusing attention selectively
- comparing nonverbal and verbal cues
- learning and using language "chunks"
- practicing new language
- using context to construct meaning

Progress Indicators

- test appropriate use of new language, phrases, and structures
- understand verbal directions by comparing them with nonverbal cues
- imitate a classmates' response to a teacher's question or directions
- associate realia or diagrams with written labels to learn vocabulary or construct meaning
- practice recently learned language by teaching a peer

PROCEDURE

- I introduce this activity by holding up a see-through box of "People Colors" crayons (Roylco, n.d.). I tell my students that each crayon represents one of their skin colors or tones. I explain that none of us is "black" or "white" and hold up those separate crayons, putting them to my skin as I am talking. This truly gets their attention.

- Next, I have the students sit on the rug, and we read a story about faces. Two good books to use are *Here are my Hands* (Martin, 1992) and *People* (Spier, 1994). Both have wonderful pictures of skin tones and face parts. I stop throughout the story and ask children to point out the face parts mentioned, such as by having

I have a rich skin color, so in order to use my own skin color as an example, I had to mix a few crayon colors together. Many of my students did the same during the activity because some of them could not find one crayon that matched their skin colors. This showed me their awareness of their different skin tones and their eagerness to find the closest match.

Face-Shaped Paper

them put their fingers on their noses or mouths. Occasionally I ask specific students to identify a face part from the book or from my face in order to check vocabulary knowledge.

- I then have the students sit six to a table, each with a box of crayons. Their task is to find the crayons that are closest to their skin tones. I start by doing my own as an example. Students find their crayons and help those who have difficulty. I usually allow 5–10 minutes for this part of the activity.

- Next, I introduce students to the faces, which are available in the *All About Me* craft kit (Roylco, n.d.). These are cutouts in various shades similar to the crayons. I give each table several cutout faces of each shade and tell the students to match their crayons with the face of the closest color. Having the crayon that matches the same color as the face reinforces for the students that they have made the right choice for their skin tones. It also promotes conversation about what they are going to draw on this face cutout.

- I then give the students additional crayons in different colors and tell them to draw their own faces. I review the parts of a face as they point to them, to promote further clarity for students still having trouble. Students then can start drawing and going to the mirror as much as needed for help drawing their faces on paper. One student's face-shaped paper is shown above.

This activity involves continuous monitoring and a lot of teacher interaction with all students. ESOL students and special education students often need one-on-one support from the teacher or a student partner.

Pre-K ESL Evaluation Form

ESL Skills

Listening   _____

Speaking   _____

Reading   _____

Writing   _____

Behavior   _____

Work Habits

Works independently   _____

Follows directions   _____

Evaluation Key

S	Satisfactory
N	Needs improvement
U	Unable to accomplish
N/A	Not applicable

Comments

Teacher _____ Date _____

Parent Signature _____ Date _____

ASSESSMENT

I assess throughout the entire activity by observing teacher-student interactions as well as students' final products. I also observe student-student interactions as a way of identifying students with more advanced English proficiency. I record my observations on the pre-K ESL evaluation form shown above.

Getting to Know You: Worksheet and Photograph

PURPOSE: TO ENGAGE STUDENTS AND TEACHER IN DISCUSSING PERSONALITY TRAITS; TO IDENTIFY LIKENESSES AND DIFFERENCES AMONG OTHER STUDENTS AND TEACHERS.

I introduce this activity to my students at the beginning of the school year, usually during the first week. I tell them that I want to get to know them better and that I need them to help me by telling me more about themselves. This promotes conversation and allows me to assess what each student knows in English.

This activity can be adapted to any grade level. This worksheet is the one that I use with my students, but other teachers can create similar ones according to the needs and interests of their students. It is a good idea to have the worksheets laminated before they are displayed to protect them from wear and tear and to keep them intact.

PROCEDURE

- I work with students individually to fill out the "Getting to Know You" worksheet shown on page 9. I ask them questions such as "When is your birthday?" and write down their answers. During the last 15 minutes of class, I help them share this information with one or two other students. This way, each child in the small group has time to share, listen, and ask questions.

- The next day, I bring students together, and we compare answers. This is a good time for expressing ideas and engaging in student-student and student-teacher conversations. Students share phrases or sentences describing something about themselves to their classmates.

- Then I take a picture of each child with an instant camera. After we look at the pictures and talk about them, I tape their pictures onto the corners of the "Getting to Know You" worksheets and post them on the door outside the classroom.

> The camera is a good classroom tool because children love to look at their pictures. They seem proud of their accomplishment and want to know more about how they are like and different from other students in the classroom. Overall, this activity is a great icebreaker and promotes socialization for 4-year-old children.

Goal 1, Standard 1 **To use English to communicate in social settings: Students will use English to participate in social interactions.**

Descriptors

- sharing and requesting information
- expressing ideas
- engaging in conversations

Progress Indicators

- volunteer information and respond to questions about self and family
- elicit information and ask clarification questions
- clarify and restate information as needed
- indicate interests, opinions, or preferences

ASSESSMENT

Assessment is ongoing throughout the entire procedure. I evaluate student-teacher interactions as well as student-student interactions. Oral communication and use of words are the key assessment measures in this activity. Most of the time I use my ongoing assessment checklist, Assessment on the Run, which is shown on page 10. This is a quick way for me to record and refer to what students know and what I am discovering during this activity and others throughout the unit and the rest of the school term.

Getting to Know You

Meet:

Birthday:_____

Age: _____

From: _____

Grade: _____

School: _____

Languages I speak:

_____

_____

_____

Favorite Things:

Food: _____

Snack:_____

Dessert: _____

Sports:_____

Color: _____

Music:_____

Hobbies:_____

Subject: _____

Movie: _____

Day: _____

Creating a Book

PURPOSE: TO PROMOTE STUDENTS' AWARENESS OF THEIR OWN AND OTHERS' EVERYDAY LIVES.

I talk with my students about the things I do every day and the people I see on a regular basis. I then show them my "All About Me: Marvelous, Magnificent Me" book. This is a good way to share experiences I have had with my students as well as to show them what they need to do to create their own books. I read each page of the book and describe the pictures I drew to go with my sentences at the bottom of every page.

A lot of parent interaction can be used with this particular activity. Children can take their books home to have their parents help them draw pictures showing more of their cultural identity. I have varied this assignment in the past by having students color pictures of their houses or pictures of their families playing a favorite game together. Before this activity, I always make sure every student in my class is able to relate as much as possible to this assignment and to complete it. I view the class as a whole and decide what specific assignments are best.

Assessment on the Run

Alphabet

a	b	c	d	e	f	g	h	i	j	k	l	m
n	o	p	q	r	s	t	u	v	w	x	y	z
A	B	C	D	E	F	G	H	I	J	K	L	M
N	O	P	Q	R	S	T	U	V	W	X	Y	Z

Numbers

1	2	3	4	5	6	7	8	9	10	11	12	13
14	15	16	17	18	19	20						

Colors

red green blue black brown yellow orange white purple pink

Oral Language Examples

Words and phrases:

Sentences:

Dates of Assessments: _____ _____ _____ _____

_____ _____ _____ _____

Teacher's Name _____

PROCEDURE

- I put several pieces of blank paper together, fold them in half, and staple them along the fold to form a minibook similar to mine. I place a blank book at each student's seat. I ask students to think about themselves or about the thing they like to do the most and to draw that image on the front of their books. They also write their names at the top of the front cover. Although most students still do not know how to write their names, I always remind them that they have excellent handwriting and that they do a great job with their names, whether or not they are really legible yet.

My ESOL students and special education students needed a bit more guidance during this activity. A buddy, teacher, or teacher's assistant helps those students who are having trouble getting started.

Goal 2, Standard 1 **To use English to achieve academically in all content areas: Students will use English to interact in the classroom.**

Descriptors

- following oral and written directions, implicit and explicit
- negotiating and managing interaction to accomplish tasks
- expressing likes, dislikes, and needs

Progress Indicators

- draw an appropriate picture in response to a teacher's directions
- ask a teacher to restate or simplify directions
- ask for assistance with a task

Student "All About Me" Book Cover

- I remind them to do only the front cover and nothing else. (With these young children, it is a good idea to make extra books in case someone does not quite follow these directions.) After they are finished with their cover pictures, I collect the books to keep and share with the class before the next page is done. Students are encouraged to talk about what they have drawn. One student's "All About Me" book cover is shown on page 11.

- The remaining pages of the book are finished at various times throughout the unit. When they are complete, the children present them to the class.

ASSESSMENT

I do my assessment several different ways for this activity.

- Observing assignments during class is my most informative way to evaluate each student. It helps me see if they understand the goal for the book.

- Parent interaction is also useful because the parents usually tell me if their children are having trouble with any aspect of the assignment.

- Another method of assessment I use comes from students' journal writings. My students "write" in journals every day, and to see their writing improve daily is very rewarding. These journals allow me to see where students were in writing on the first day of school and how they are progressing. This is my most reliable source for assessing students' writing.

Body Parts and Clothing

PURPOSE: TO IDENTIFY BODY PARTS AND NAMES FOR CLOTHES.

This activity generates a lot of class participation as well as accomplishing the curriculum goals set by the school district. Learning body parts can be a difficult task for our children, but they need to know them before entering kindergarten.

Goal 1, Standard 2 To use English to communicate in social settings: Students will interact in, through, and with spoken and written English for personal expression and enjoyment.

Descriptors
- describing, reading about, or participating in a favorite activity
- sharing social and cultural traditions and values
- expressing personal needs, feelings, and ideas

Progress Indicators
- draw body parts and clothes on paper
- ask information questions
- talk about favorite clothes

PROCEDURE

- I introduce this activity with an enjoyable song, "Head, Shoulders, Knees, and Toes." I usually sing the song slowly four or five times, doing each movement with the words so that all of my students can touch the specific body part while singing the song.

- After the song, the children sit on the floor, and I show them a paper cut in the shape of a small body. I point to the main body parts on the cutout and ask the students to tell me the name of each part. We go over this three times, which allows all students to have a turn to participate. I then draw students' attention to the fact that the bodies on their papers have no eyes, hands, or toes. I tell them that it is our job to draw the body parts on the papers.

"All About Me" Body Drawing

- I tell children to pretend that the body shape on their papers is their own and that they need to draw their body parts on it. I guide the students back to their seats and have them use crayons to draw their body parts on their own papers. One student's "All About Me" body drawing is shown on page 13.

- *Wrist*, *knee*, and *ankle* are usually very difficult words for my students to remember. It is a good idea to continuously repeat the names of the body parts while the students are participating in the activity so they will remember to draw them. After about 5–10 minutes, I review the body parts again with the entire group.

- I then introduce the next part of the activity, mentioning that these drawings are good but that now we need to add some clothes to them. I help students name the articles of clothing that I am wearing. Then I ask various students if they want to share what they are wearing. As they do, I tell them to draw what they are wearing on their papers. Because they are drawing themselves, I can get an idea of what they like to wear.

This clothing activity may be too advanced for some students to do right away, so one-on-one help is often needed. But as the unit continues, clothing is mentioned a great deal. Students usually grasp the names of most common clothing articles with this regular exposure and review.

Assessment

After the children have finished coloring, they bring their papers to the floor and sit waiting to share with the group what they have done. They talk about the body parts they colored and what they are wearing that day. In assessing, I listen mainly to the oral language as well as examine their drawings. This is a good independent activity that shows students' progress and comprehension. I keep paper and pen nearby for jotting down new words the children use in their descriptions.

Learning Names and Letters

Purpose: To recognize and identify letters in students' names and write them on paper.

I introduce this activity with students as a whole group and then work with them individually during center time.

Procedure

- Parent Involvement: Before beginning this activity, I send a note home to get parent input. I ask parents to send in written information about why they named their children specific names.

- We begin this activity by reviewing the letters of the alphabet and singing the ABC song. Then we go back to the letter *A*, and every child whose name begins with *A* stands. By the time we get to the letter *Z*, everyone is standing.

- I tell my students that we are going to work with them on writing their names. I always explain how important names are because they tell others more about you. For example, my first name, Carla, came from my aunt Clara. The two names sound similar, yet they are different. My aunt was a nice person, so I try to be like her. This example usually sparks conversations. Then I read the information that the parents sent in about their children's names.

- During center time, I call two or three children at a time to a separate table. I ask them to write their names at the bottom of a paper. After doing so, they draw something at the top of the paper that shows their personalities. I give them several examples, such as "riding a bike with a friend and being friendly," or "helping out a friend who fell down or is sad." I want them to remember all the nice things they do and to think about them when someone says their names.

This is a very flexible activity. I do not put time limits on it because it is done during center time. However, it can also be done as a whole-group activity.

Goal 2, Standard 3 To use English to achieve academically in all content areas: Students will use appropriate learning strategies to construct and apply academic knowledge.

Descriptors

- evaluating one's own success in a completed learning task
- recognizing the need for and seeking assistance appropriately from others (e.g., teachers, peers, specialists, community members)
- knowing when to use native language resources (human and material) to promote understanding

Progress Indicators

- use verbal and nonverbal cues to know when to pay attention
- make pictures to check comprehension of a story or process
- take risks with language
- rephrase, explain, revise, and expand oral or written information to check comprehension
- seek more knowledgeable others with whom to consult to advance understanding

ASSESSMENT

This is a good activity for independent student work. The task is usually easy to do with small children, but there will always be students who need extra teacher support. Assessment is ongoing throughout the entire activity through student-teacher interactions and comprehension checks.

Identifying Role Models

PURPOSE: TO IDENTIFY COMMUNITY ROLE MODELS AS WELL AS THE CAREERS CHILDREN WOULD LIKE TO HAVE WHEN THEY GET OLDER.

I always begin this activity with examples of community helpers. A good book to get this activity going is *Help!* (Graham, 1994). It is about a little girl who gets her fingers stuck in a gum ball machine, and many community helpers come to her aid.

Goal 1, Standard 2   To use English to communicate in social settings: Students will interact in, through, and with spoken and written English for personal expression and enjoyment.

Descriptors

- describing, reading about, or participating in a favorite activity
- expressing personal needs, feelings, and ideas

Progress Indicators

- listen to and respond to books
- recount events of interest
- ask information questions for personal reasons
- discuss and draw occupations

PROCEDURE

- I start the lesson by having the students look at the cover of the book and make predictions about what will happen in the story. We read the story and review our predictions to see who was right. I point out the many community helpers who helped Katie in the story and ask my students to rename them for me. As they do, I write them on the chalkboard (or an easel). I ask them if they want to be any of these helpers when they grow up, and we discuss what these helpers do.

- I start reading *When I Grow Up* (Mayer, 1991), which leads into a discussion of what students want to be when they grow up. They then go to their seats for their assignment, which is to draw what they want to be when they grow up. When they finish, they tell me why they want to be this person, and I write it at the bottom of their drawings.

- Parent Involvement/Adaptation: Teachers can also involve parents in this assignment. After reading the story *Help!* (Graham, 1994) or another story, I send a note home to parents asking them to discuss community helpers in further detail with their children and to discuss how they themselves have helped their communities. Parents send in notes the next day, and students share them with the class. Or parents can help their children decide what they want to be when they grow up and help them draw a picture of it to take to school the next day.

ASSESSMENT

Assessment for this activity is through class participation and observation. Many students sit quietly and do not speak, so I call on them and help them if needed. Most of my ESOL students do very well with this activity.

Creating and Sharing a Family Album

PURPOSE: TO DISCUSS ORALLY AND IN WRITING STUDENTS' FAMILY MEMBERS AND FAMILY HISTORIES.

This activity is very structured, but it is one of my favorites for ESOL children and their families.

Goal 1, Standard 1 **To use English to communicate in social settings: Students will use English to participate in social interactions.**

Descriptors

- sharing and requesting information
- expressing needs, feelings, and ideas
- engaging in conversations

Progress Indicators

- volunteer information and respond to questions about self and family
- elicit information and ask clarification questions
- clarify and restate information as needed
- indicate interests, opinions, or preferences related to class projects

---

PROCEDURE

- I begin this activity by sending a note home with the following questions. But first I read the questions to my students in case their parents cannot read English.

    Who lives in your house?

    Who takes care of the children?

    Who cooks for the family?

    Do you have any animals?

    Can you send in a picture of your house or family?

- Students take the papers home. Even if their parents do not speak English, the students usually remember what I read to them and can translate the questions for their parents.

- Students almost always bring back the answers the very next day. With this information as a foundation, we start our family album. I share pictures and drawings from my family album with the entire class. After all children have shared the information they brought from home, we start on our albums.

- My students love to paint. I give them large sheets of paper and ask them to create family portraits for their parents. At the end of the 4 weeks, we will compile all of their work from this unit and send it home in the form of an album.

Parent involvement is essential for this lesson to succeed. If some children do not know or have this information to share, that must be respected. However, the pleasure of creating the picture for the album is universal because when the children leave school, they have something to take home to show to those who take care of them.

ASSESSMENT

I assess this activity by evaluating oral and artistic communication. Because this is an identity awareness activity, I focus only on the communicative aspect.

Numbers and Colors: Identifying Favorites

PURPOSE: TO IDENTIFY COLORS AND NUMBERS; TO DISCUSS FAVORITES USING SIMPLE AND COMPOUND COMPLETE SENTENCES.

This activity uses single- and double-slot **substitution drills**. It works as a great curriculum assessment piece and is also quite enjoyable.

Goal 2, Standard 3 **To use English to achieve academically in all content areas: Students will use appropriate learning strategies to construct and apply academic knowledge.**

Descriptors

- focusing attention selectively
- applying self-monitoring and self-corrective strategies to build and expand a knowledge base
- actively connecting new information to information previously learned
- imitating the behaviors of native English speakers to complete tasks successfully

Progress Indicators

- use verbal and nonverbal cues to know when to pay attention
- rehearse and visualize information

PROCEDURE

- I ask the children to look at posters in the room with the colors and the numbers 1 to 20 on them. I say the sentence, "I like the number 1," and they repeat it. We proceed until we get to the number 20, and then do the same with the colors red, orange, blue, green, black, white, and yellow. After these sentences have been repeated, we say the sentence, "I don't like the number 1," and proceed with the colors in the same pattern.
- After all sentences are complete, I say, "I like the number 1, but I don't like the color blue." Students repeat it, and I continue this pattern with several

more sentences, substituting number and color words. We have now changed from a single-slot substitution to a double-slot substitution.

- Children are then asked randomly to tell what numbers they like or dislike, and then what colors. Teacher direction is a must in the beginning, but students soon catch on and say the sentences independently as the lesson progresses.

ASSESSMENT

We review the sentences and substitutions the next day to check comprehension. I ask students to draw or paint their favorite colors and numbers. This can be put in their cumulative folders as a good resource to indicate comprehension of these concepts.

Informal Oral Language Test

PURPOSE: TO IDENTIFY LETTERS (IN ORDER AND RANDOMLY), COLORS, SHAPES, NUMBERS, PICTURES OF OBJECTS, AND INITIAL SOUNDS.

This lesson consists of an assessment tool used for report cards, and it provides a lot of valuable information. I begin the assessment toward the end of the unit and finish it by the end of the grading period. This helps me evaluate where my children are and where I need to take them in the next unit and the next grading period.

> *Goal 2, Standard 2* To use English to achieve academically in content areas: Students will use English to obtain, process, construct, and provide subject matter information in spoken and written form.
>
> ### Descriptors
> - retelling information
> - selecting, connecting, and explaining information
> - understanding and producing technical vocabulary according to content area
> - demonstrating knowledge through application in a variety of contexts
>
> ### Progress Indicators
> - identify and associate written symbols with words
> - define, compare, and classify objects

PROCEDURE

- I explain to the students before they go to centers that I will be pulling them out one by one for a talk. I say, "This will allow me to find out what you already know and how smart you are. We have been doing many things about ourselves and telling each other about what kind of people we are, but I also need to let everyone know how much you have learned in this unit."

- During center time, I call children individually and ask them questions from the Informal Oral ESL Test, which is shown on page 20. The test consists of two pages on which the teacher records results for each student, plus five

Informal Oral ESL Test

Student Name _____

Date _____

School _____

Teacher _____

Circle the Correct Answer:

I.   Recites the alphabet in order.

II. Tracks through the alphabet in serial order.

A	B	C	D	E	F	G	H	I	J	K	L	M
N	O	P	Q	R	S	T	U	V	W	X	Y	Z

III. Recognizes the letters of the alphabet (give randomly).

A	B	C	D	E	F	G	H	I	J	K	L	M
N	O	P	Q	R	S	T	U	V	W	X	Y	Z
a	b	c	d	e	f	g	h	i	j	k	l	m
n	o	p	q	r	s	t	u	v	w	x	y	z

IV. Recognizes colors.

red	brown	green	yellow	white
blue	orange	purple	black	pink

V.   Recognizes basic shapes.

triangle   circle   square   rectangle

VI. Recognizes numbers (give randomly).

1   2   3   4   5   6   7   8   9   10   11   12

VII. Understands number concepts (example: How many stars do you see?).

2   3   4   5   6   7   8   9   10

VIII. Recognizes pictures (check if correct).

bird _____   car _____   duck _____   fish _____   ghost _____   house _____
jump rope _____   kite _____   lamp _____   monkey _____   necklace _____
pencil _____   rabbit _____   sandwich _____   telephone _____
violin _____   watch _____   yo-yo _____

IX. Knows initial sounds (check if correct).

t __   r __   g __   w __   d __   l __   c __   f __   h __   n __   b __
s __   p __   j __   v __   k __   t __   m __

Writing Sample

_____
_____
_____
_____

Comments

_____   _____
_____
_____
_____

pages of student prompts (see below and p. 22). This helps me assess letter knowledge; color, shape, and number recognition; basic vocabulary; initial sound recognition; and students' learning styles.

ASSESSMENT

The information from the test, as well as my observations while giving it, are the assessment tools I use during this activity. I do not expect all the students to know all this information at the beginning of the year, but this gives me a starting point. I go back to this comprehensive assessment tool several times during the year.

Student Prompts for Informal Oral Test

How many stars do you see?

Directions: Ask the student to count the stars and tell you the total number counted.

What numbers are these?

1   3   6
9   11   5
4   2   8
7   10   12

Directions: Arrange numbers randomly. Ask the student to point to the numbers as you say them aloud.

continued on p. 22

Student Prompts for Informal Oral Test, *continued*

What letters are these?

A C E G I K M O Q S U W Y B
D F H J L N P R T V X Z
b d f h j l n p r t v x z a c
e g i k m o q s u w y

Directions: Arrange the letters randomly. Ask the student to point to the letters as you say them aloud.

Can you identify the colors?

| (red) | (white) | (blue) |

| (green) | (yellow) | (orange) | (black) |

Directions: Ask the student to color in each square according to the oral prompt (e.g., "blue"). As an additional check, show the student something blue and ask the student to name the color.

What shape is this?

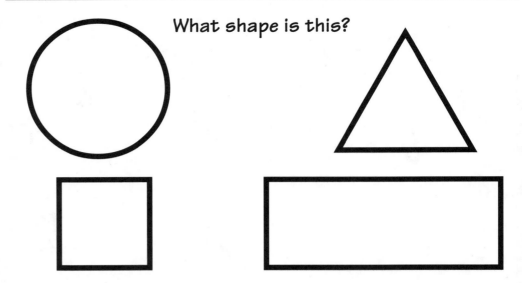

Directions: Point to each shape and ask the student to identify it. If the student is unable to identify the shape, prompt the student by asking a question, such as "Which one is a triangle?"

Conclusion

Usually by the end of this unit, I see a big difference in almost all of my children. They show more self-confidence and more confidence communicating with each other. It is such a feeling of joy to see them so happy and proud of who they are and of the new language they are now beginning to understand. As an ESL teacher, that is the best feeling one can have.

RESOURCES AND REFERENCES

Children's Literature

Cheltenham Elementary School Kindergartners. (1991). We are all alike—we are all different. *New York: Scholastic.*
> *Created by children, this book shows children that they are all different in appearance yet still are all the same.*

Davidson, A. (1990). *The lion and the mouse.* New York: Scholastic.
> *This book is about friendship and trust. It is a great book for promoting friendships.*

Fox, M., & Staub, L. (Illustrator). (1997). *Whoever you are.* New York: Harcourt Brace.
> *This simple story delivers a powerful message: On the outside, children may look different all over the world, but on the inside, feelings and emotions are the same. This book promotes multicultural understanding and awareness of self and emotions.*

Graham, A. (1994). *Help!* New York: Scholastic.
> *This book is about a little girl who needs help with a gum machine. All of the local community helpers come and try to rescue her.*

Martin, B. (1992). *Here are my hands.* New York: Harcourt Brace.
> *This is a rhyming book about body parts.*

Mayer, M. (1991). *When I grow up.* New York: Golden Books.
> *This book is about a child who is wondering what he will do when he grows up because there are so many important jobs in the world.*

Raschka, C. (1993). *Yo! Yes?* New York: Orchard.
> *This book is about two young boys communicating through one-word phrases. They understand each other through body language. It is a good book for beginning-level ESOL students to enjoy.*

Reiser, L. (1993). *Margaret and Margarita.* New York: Scholastic.
> *Two young girls meet in a park and realize that they speak different languages. However, by the time they leave the park, they learn to listen to and understand one another.*

Spier, P. (1994). *People.* New York: Scholastic.
> *This book describes various types of people in the world.*

Other Classroom Materials

Conn Beall, P., & Nipp, S. H. (1994). *Wee sing around the world* [Audiotape]. Los Angeles, CA: Price Stern Sloan.
> *This audiotape and book set has various songs from around the world performed in English and other languages.*

Keyes, J. R. (1998). *The Oxford picture dictionary for kids.* New York: Oxford University Press.
> *This 700-word dictionary is designed around pictures that tell stories about five different families.*

Roylco. (n.d.). *All about me* [Craft kit]. Sanborn, NY: Roylco.
> *This craft kit contains colored paper and crayons to promote multicultural awareness among young children.*

Schaffer, F. (1994). *Easy picture words, Sets 1 & 2* [Flash cards]. New York: Frank Schaffer.

Usborne's animated first thousand words in English and Spanish [CD-ROM]. (1997). New York: Scholastic.
> *This Windows- and Macintosh-compatible CD-ROM for children ages 5–7 helps build vocabulary.*

Teacher Resources

Donaldson, J .P. (1999). *Transcultural picture word list for teaching English to children from any of 35 language backgrounds* (2nd ed.). Holmes Beach, FL: Learning Publications.
> *This book contains picture word lists that can help teachers communicate with students and families from many different cultural backgrounds.*

Moore, H. (1994). *The multilingual translator: Words and phrases in 35 languages to help you communicate with students of diverse backgrounds* (2nd ed.). Holmes Beach, FL: Learning Publications.
> *The word lists, information about languages, and examples of letters to parents will be of great help to teachers who need to communicate with non-English-speaking families.*

Newport News Public Schools. (1998). *A journey through a multicultural world curriculum guide.* Newport News, VA: Author. (Available from Newport News Public Schools, 2465 Warwick Boulevard, Newport News, VA 23606)

Newport News Public Schools ESL Department. (1991). *ESL handbook for school personnel working with students of limited English proficiency.* Newport News, VA: Author. (Available from Newport News Public Schools, 2465 Warwick Boulevard, Newport News, VA 23606)

Newport News Public Schools Revision Committee. (1994). *Title I first step curriculum guide.* Newport News, VA: Author. (Available from Newport News Public Schools, 2465 Warwick Boulevard, Newport News, VA 23606)

Ramsey, P. G. (1998). *Teaching and learning in a diverse world: Multicultural education for young children* (2nd ed.). New York: Teachers College Press.
> *The author wrote this second edition to expand on children's understanding of multicultural issues in their environments.*

Spangenberg-Urbschat, K., & Pritchard, R. (1994). *Kids come in all languages: Reading instruction for ESL students.* Newark, DE: International Reading Association.
> *This is a guide for teachers of ESOL children on instructional practices in the classroom and how to implement them.*

Tabors, P. (1997). *One child, two languages: A guide for preschool educators of children learning English as a second language.* Baltimore, MD: Paul H. Brookes.
> *The author describes the rising number of preschool ESOL children in the United States and shares research and other information with educators about how to better serve these children.*

TESOL. (1997). *ESL standards for pre-K–12 students.* Alexandria, VA: Author.
> *This book contains the standards, descriptors, and progress indicators used in this unit, plus classroom vignettes and other useful information.*

Titone, R. (1990). *Bilingual education as a big game.* New York: Helen Doron Early English.
> *This author describes the importance of learning two languages and the positive effect it has on lives.*

UNIT 2
Making Bread Together

SONIA JAMES

Introduction

As you walk through the door of Jennifer Anderson's kindergarten classroom, you notice the happy faces of the children actively playing in learning centers throughout the room. Some are busy painting pictures, others are building with blocks, listening to stories on tape, or developing their own writing skills.

The activities and materials in each learning center relate to the food-group unit the class is studying. Through these activities, the students develop social interaction skills and academic skills, which are essential for the first year of formal schooling.

Jennifer's kindergarten class consists of a diverse group of 24 students. Nine of these students are designated English language learners because their primary language is not English. The student population of the class consists of European American, African American, Bosnian, Albanian, and Hispanic children.

The mainstream classroom teacher and I, the ESL teacher, collaborate closely to design a curriculum that meets the needs of all of the students. Based on the high number of limited English proficient students in the class, we decided to use an inclusion model of instruction rather than an ESL pullout model. We felt that with two of us working together in one classroom, all of the students would benefit.

Context

Grade level: Kindergarten

English proficiency levels: Mixed, from nonspeakers to orally proficient

Native languages of students: English, Spanish, Bosnian, Albanian

Focus of instruction: Beginning-level reading and language arts development

Type of class: Mainstream classroom with collaboration and support from ESL teacher

Length of unit: Approximately 2 weeks

Unit Overview

This unit is part of a science theme that covers the four basic food groups. To teach this theme, we designed a curriculum that integrates science skills and language arts. The length of time spent studying each of the food groups varies, depending on the materials and resources available and the interest of the students. The specific unit of study here focuses on the bread and cereal group. We prefer to teach this unit in the spring of the year because we can incorporate a science unit on plant growth.

This unit takes about 2 weeks to complete. In our school, we have a full-day kindergarten program. This allows us to spend more time covering the subject areas in the kindergarten curriculum. We generally spend about 1 hour per day on language arts activities. Some of the activities in the unit can be completed in 1 day, whereas others will last for 2 days. The activities can be adapted to fit other schedules.

During this unit, I plan closely with the mainstream classroom teacher to select activities that are developmentally appropriate and meet the needs of the native speakers as well as the nonnative speakers. For a collaborative model of instruction to work effectively, the mainstream classroom teacher and the ESL teacher must share in the planning process as well as in the implementation of the lesson. Common planning time during the day is best, but this is not always possible due to the ESL teacher's scheduling constraints.

Jennifer and I have found creative and flexible ways to plan. For instance, we met before the school year began to set an overall schedule of monthly themes for the year. Throughout the year we meet after school once every 2 weeks to plan specific activities and units. We feel the students benefit from our sharing of ideas. If we get an idea for an activity or unit or lesson, we write it down and share it with each other sometime during the day. The trick to joint planning is to find out what works best for you and to always be flexible.

The overall objectives for the unit are for the students to

Content

- identify different kinds of bread around the world
- gain basic knowledge of food groups

Language

- orally respond to a story in print
- practice oral language
- develop listening skills

Learning Strategy

- work in small groups to complete assignments

The unit overview on page 27 provides a graphic representation of the unit.

Standards

My decision to use an inclusion (push-in) instead of a pullout model of instruction affects my planning because I must now work closely with Jennifer, the kindergarten teacher, to plan activities for the units of study and to incorporate different sets of standards.

Before I begin planning a unit of study, I sit down and review the standards, descriptors, and progress indicators in *ESL Standards for Pre-K–12 Students* (TESOL, 1997)

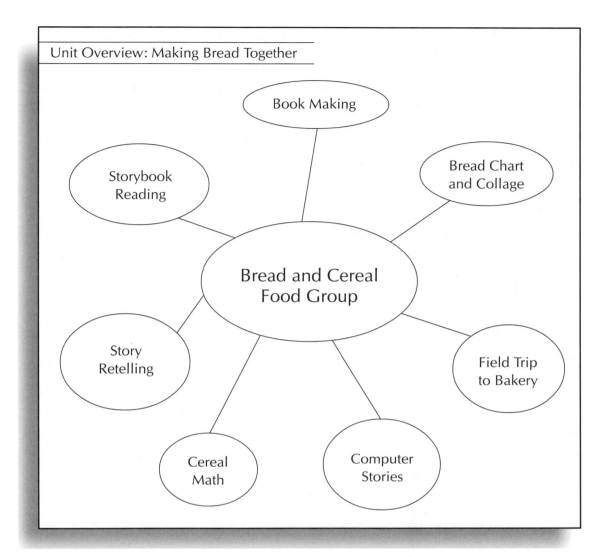

Unit Overview: Making Bread Together

- Book Making
- Storybook Reading
- Bread Chart and Collage
- Bread and Cereal Food Group
- Story Retelling
- Field Trip to Bakery
- Cereal Math
- Computer Stories

to get them fresh in my mind. I also review the state curriculum guidelines for the kindergarten content areas and the program of studies for kindergarten to see how they fit with the ESL standards. Then I meet with the kindergarten teacher to plan the activities for a particular unit of study. Jennifer comes to this planning process with a strong background knowledge of the requirements for the kindergarten curriculum.

As we plan collaboratively, we seek creative ways to actively involve our students in the learning process while also meeting the ESL standards and state guidelines. With both of us sharing thoughts and ideas, we feel more assured of accomplishing this task than if we were working alone, without the benefit of each other's knowledge and experience.

Because we include the ESL standards and the kindergarten guidelines during the planning stages, assessment becomes a natural part of the instructional day. Informal assessment occurs daily as we watch all children interact and develop language skills during each task. Formal assessment occurs when we view the finished product for each task or assignment. The terminology of the ESL standards facilitates assessment. Through the wording of the standards, descriptors, and especially the progress indicators, it is fairly easy to determine if the student has met a particular standard. As long as I have referred to these standards as my guide for planning and assessment, I am assured of addressing all the English language development skills of my students.

For kindergarten-age ESOL students, the main focus of development is on oral language skills. We assess students by listening to them and observing them during their daily responses in class. We keep samples of their daily writing or picture work. Keeping these over a period of time allows us to see if improvement is occurring.

Activities

To attract the students to the unit, we display different pictures of breads and cereals around the room. For this unit, the following materials are required:

- **big book** version of "The Little Red Hen" (McCloskey, Hooper, Linse, & Schottman, 1996)
- small versions of the story on the bookshelf for the students to read during center time
- magazines with pictures of food
- parental permission forms for field trip
- computer programs with stories about bread and cereal
- cereal that can be sorted, counted, and grouped by color and shape, such as Froot Loops or Lucky Charms

Storybook Reading: "The Little Red Hen"

To introduce the unit, we read the story "The Little Red Hen" (McCloskey et al., 1996). This is a favorite story for children of all ages, and versions of it exist in other countries. Sharing these versions adds a component of diversity while including all of the students in the learning process. We have available in the classroom reading library other versions of "The Little Red Hen" for students to read.

Goal 1, Standard 1   **To use English to communicate in social settings: Students will use English to participate in social interactions.**

Descriptors
- sharing and requesting information
- expressing needs, feelings, and ideas
- engaging in conversations

Progress Indicators
- engage listener's attention verbally and nonverbally
- clarify and restate information as needed
- describe feelings and emotions

> **Goal 2, Standard 2**   To use English to achieve academically in all content areas: Students will use English to obtain, process, construct, and provide subject matter information in spoken and written form.

Descriptors

- listening to, speaking, reading, and writing about subject matter information
- retelling information
- representing information visually and interpreting information presented visually

Progress Indicators

- gather and organize materials needed to complete a task
- use contextual clues
- orally answer questions about a story read aloud
- copy title and illustrate favorite part of story

PROCEDURE

- We get the students settled on the carpet, ready to listen. I sit on the carpet close to the ESOL students so that I can explain things in the story when needed. Jennifer begins to read aloud to the whole class the big book of "The Little Red Hen."

- As Jennifer reads the story, she stops periodically to ask the students questions and also to ask them to retell what is happening up to this point. I interact with the ESOL students to make sure they understand the components of the story being told. I encourage them to respond to Jennifer's questions and help them answer.

- After Jennifer finishes reading the story, she asks questions to check oral comprehension. She uses different question types that cover various degrees of difficulty to give all students the chance to respond with success. I also notice that she uses proper questioning techniques. Some questions include:

    Who is the main character in the story?

    What did she want to make?

    Did anyone help her make the bread?

    Why did the other animals not help?

    Who wanted to eat the bread?

    The ESOL students are able to answer the questions either by responding orally or by pointing to the picture in the book that answers the question.

- After discussing the story, we ask the students to return to their seats and illustrate their favorite part of the story. They copy the title of the story onto their papers as best they can. "The Little Red Hen" is written on the board in big bold letters for all students to see. I work with the ESOL students to review the story, help them choose their favorite part, and draw it on their papers. I find that drawings done by the ESOL students are not much different from those done by the rest of the class. Two students' drawings are shown below.

Students' Drawings

Little Red Hen

bread

Planting wheat

Little Red Hen

ASSESSMENT

Assessment is done informally by listening to the story discussion while in the large group and by looking at students' illustrations of the story. In a scoring rubric, we are looking for the following items:

> Did students clarify and restate information?
>
> Did they represent information visually?
>
> Did they gather information to respond to the questions?

These questions connect to the descriptors and progress indicators from the identified standards for the activity.

Book Making

The entire class works together to write a class book entitled *I Like Bread.* Each student is responsible for writing and illustrating one page of the book.

Goal 2, Standard 2 **To use English to achieve academically in all content areas: Students will use English to obtain, process, construct, and provide subject matter information in spoken and written form.**

Descriptors

- listening to, speaking, reading, and writing about subject matter information
- gathering information orally and in writing
- demonstrating knowledge through application in a variety of contexts

Progress Indicators

- gather and organize the appropriate materials needed to complete a task
- use contextual cues
- identify and associate written symbols with words
- illustrate sentence to indicate comprehension
- read class book

PROCEDURE

- We begin the **book making** activity with all of the students seated on the carpet for story time. Jennifer and I lead a review in which we name and discuss the different bread types. We have the students refer to the charts and pictures hanging around the room. After this discussion, we introduce the idea that our class is going to write its own book.

- I read the story *Everybody Bakes Bread* (Dooley, 1996) to the class. After the story, Jennifer discusses the different parts of the book, while I show the class where the parts are located. We point out features such as the title, story, illustrations, author, and illustrator, and tell students that our book will also need the same parts.

- Jennifer writes the following sentence on the board for the students to copy on their page: *I like to eat* _____. Students write the sentence, filling in the blank with the kinds of bread they like to eat. Then they illustrate their sentences by drawing a picture of the bread they named. For students who are not ready to write on their own, I use a yellow highlighter to write the words on their paper. Then they are able to trace the words.

- When all of the pages are complete, I laminate them and bind them together into one big book. We read the book to the class. Afterwards, the book stays on the bookshelf for the students to read during center time.

ASSESSMENT

Assessment for this activity is informal and formal. Informally, we interact with the students as they work on writing their pages. We check to see if they understand what they are writing and drawing about. Formally, we have the book for all to see.

Class Bread Chart and Collage

In this activity, the students help create a chart listing different types of bread (shown on p. 33). They then discuss the breads with which they are familiar. This activity provides a good opportunity to highlight the cultural diversity of the class by discussing breads from the ESOL students' native countries. After listing the different types of breads, Jennifer and I help the students look through magazines to find pictures of types of bread. Together, the class makes a large collage that we hang in the hallway to share with others in the school.

> *Goal 1, Standard 3* **To use English to communicate in social settings: Students will use learning strategies to extend their communicative competence.**
>
> ### Descriptors
> - practicing new language
> - listening to and imitating how others use English
> - exploring alternative ways of saying things
> - selecting different media to help understand language
>
> ### Progress Indicators
> - understand verbal directions by comparing them with nonverbal cues
> - imitate a classmate's response to a teacher's question or directions
> - test appropriate use of new vocabulary, phrases, and structures

PROCEDURE

- We begin by calling the students to come and sit on the carpet for large-group time. We review the story from the previous day and ask the students what they know about breads. Jennifer and I take turns asking questions and responding to and elaborating on the answers of the students.

- We read aloud the story *Bread, Bread, Bread* (Morris, 1989) to introduce this activity and give students vocabulary for different breads from around the world.

- We tell the class that we want them to name all the different types of breads they can think of. We put a large piece of lined paper on the board on which to write their responses. We ask the students questions to get them thinking. Here are some of the questions we use:

  What do you put a hot dog on?

  What do you eat with spaghetti?

  What do you put a sandwich on? What color is it?

  What do you eat for breakfast in a bowl?

  As the students name various breads or cereals, we write their responses on the lined paper under the appropriate heading.

- After the word chart on breads and cereals is completed, we ask the students to look through magazines to find pictures of different breads and cereals. We help the children paste the pictures on a large piece of paper (e.g., long newsprint) to make a collage to hang in the hallway. This allows other students in the school to see what is happening in the kindergarten classroom.

> This activity gives the ESOL students the opportunity to share with their fellow classmates something about foods from their native countries and cultures. It also allows them to practice developing the social interaction skills needed to communicate this information.

ASSESSMENT

I watch how the ESOL students interact with their classmates while practicing their oral language skills. I also check on gross motor skills as they cut and glue their pictures. While they are working, I walk around the room to check on how well they are following oral directions. These are all forms of informal assessment. Formal assessment comes from viewing the final project and checking to see if directions were followed.

Bread and Cereal Chart	
Breads	**Cereals**
tortillas	oats
pita bread	cold cereals
white bread	oatmeal
rice cakes	
Italian bread	
muffins	
sourdough bread	
wheat bread	
rye bread	
oatmeal bread	

Field Trip to a Bakery

For this activity, we take the entire class on a field trip to a local bakery to see how bread is made. We even get to taste some bread while at the bakery. This adds an element of enrichment to the unit of study.

> ### Goal 3, Standard 3 To use English in socially and culturally appropriate ways: Students will use appropriate learning strategies to extend their communicative competence.
>
> #### Descriptors
>
> - observing and modeling how others speak and behave in a particular situation or setting
> - seeking information about appropriate language use and behavior
> - rehearsing variations for language in different social and academic settings
>
> #### Progress Indicators
>
> - observe language use and behaviors of peers in different settings
> - rehearse different ways of speaking according to the setting
> - test appropriate use of newly acquired language

Procedure

- Before beginning the unit, we arrange with a local bakery a specific day and time for the field trip, and obtain the service of a school bus. Once the day and time are set, permission slips must be obtained for all of the students. I help to ensure that the parents of the nonnative speakers understand about the field trip.

- Before leaving on the field trip, we prepare our students. Many of them have never ridden on a bus. We discuss rules for bus-riding safety. This is also a good review for our students who ride the bus to school every day. In the classroom, we arrange chairs on the carpet in the form of bus seats and visually demonstrate good bus behavior. This helps all students, native speakers and nonnative speakers alike, to understand exactly what is expected of them on the bus.

- Next, we go over the rules for good behavior while we are at the bakery. These include staying

This is a good enrichment activity for the entire class. It is always good to involve the community in the teaching of our young students whenever possible. A trip to the bakery allows the class to learn more about where bread comes from and how it is made, and provides them an opportunity to visit a location that is not familiar to everyone. While learning about the making of bread, ESOL students have a chance to view the actions and behaviors of their classmates in a different setting, which helps them learn how to interact.

together as a group, listening while others are talking, and raising hands to ask questions. We walk through the room as a group to model this behavior.

- As a follow-up to this activity, we have the class work as a large group to write a thank-you note to the bakery. The students dictate the sentences to put in the letter. I prompt the students for their responses while Jennifer writes them on a large piece of paper. After the letter is complete, all of the students sign their names at the bottom. The letter is then delivered to the bakery.

ASSESSMENT

By observing the students' behavior and actions during the field trip, we can determine how all students are interacting in a new environment and how well they have achieved this standard.

Computer Stories

We are fortunate to have access to, and be able to use on a regular basis, computer programs for students in kindergarten through sixth grade in the areas of reading skills and language arts. By using these computer programs, we are able to add to the knowledge base introduced in the classroom while the students learn basic computer skills.

The two programs we use are First Adventures Bookshelf (Computer Curriculum Corporation, 1994) and Discover English (Computer Curriculum Corporation, 1996). These are computer programs that teach basic skills to the kindergarten-age child in a way that is interesting and inviting to the student.

This computer activity allows students to develop their listening skills by hearing the story of "The Little Red Hen" again, to develop basic computer skills through hands-on practice, and to demonstrate knowledge of the story by interacting with the computer story.

I have used the First Adventures Bookshelf with my ESOL learners with much success. It is designed to keep students' attention as they learn and practice new skills. It allows them to "read" a story and complete activities relating to the story in a successful, nonthreatening environment. This success later carries over to activities in the classroom. Any learning activity that ESOL students can participate in and feel successful with is a good activity.

PROCEDURE

- We take the students to the computer lab and help them log onto the computers. We allow the ESOL students to work with a partner to help show them how to use the computers. We then guide them to First Adventures Bookshelf and help them find the story "The Little Red Hen." We allow all the students to work through the program at their own pace and help them as needed.

- While the students are listening to and reading along with the story on the computers, Jennifer and I walk around

All of the students, including the ESOL students, enjoy using computers. They especially enjoy the follow-up activity in which they get to make their own sandwich pictures, because the computer samples include breads from many different lands. It is a pleasure to watch the ESOL students share information about the breads they recognize with their native-English-speaking classmates.

Goal 1, Standard 2 To use English to communicate in social settings: Students will interact in, through, and with spoken and written English for personal expression and enjoyment.

Descriptors

- describing, reading about, or participating in a favorite activity
- expressing personal needs, feelings, and ideas

Progress Indicators

- listen to, read, watch, and respond to computer programs
- express enjoyment while playing a game
- recommend a book or computer program

Goal 2, Standard 1 To use English to achieve academically in all content areas: Students will use English to interact in the classroom.

Descriptors

- following oral and written directions
- requesting information and assistance
- asking and answering questions
- negotiating and managing interaction to accomplish tasks

Progress Indicators

- ask a teacher to restate or simplify directions
- share classroom materials and work successfully with a partner
- ask for assistance with a task

the room helping them with any questions they may have. After they finish the story, there are follow-up activities for the students to complete. This is where Jennifer and I help the most.

ASSESSMENT

Informal assessment comes from actively watching how the students work during their time in the computer lab. Formal assessment comes from a printout from the computer program itself. The printout gives information relating to how much time the students took to complete the task, which skills they practiced, and which ones they mastered. We combine the information from these two sources to get an overall picture of how the students are doing.

Cereal Math

This activity gives students the opportunity to develop basic math skills using cereal as a manipulative. The skills covered include sorting, graphing, counting, and comparing. Best of all, when the students finish the activity, they get to eat the cereal as a snack.

> **Goal 2, Standard 2** To use English to achieve academically in all content areas: Students will use English to obtain, process, construct, and provide subject matter information in spoken and written form.

Descriptors

- representing information visually and interpreting information presented visually
- demonstrating knowledge through application in a variety of contexts
- comparing and contrasting information
- analyzing, synthesizing, and inferring from information
- selecting, connecting, and explaining information

Progress Indicators

- define, compare, and classify objects according to number, shape, color, size, function, and physical characteristics
- record observations
- construct a chart or other graphic showing data

PROCEDURE

- First, we give each student a small plastic bag containing a handful of Lucky Charms cereal. Then we ask them to work with the other students at their tables to describe the cereal. We guide the discussion to include characteristics of the cereal such as size, color, and shape. I work with the ESOL students to help develop the vocabulary for these math terms.

- Next, we ask the students to group their cereal pieces either by shape or by color. The type of cereal helps to determine how to sort it. I explain to my ESOL group that sorting the cereal means putting like kinds together, and I demonstrate this for them. We discuss why they choose to group the pieces as they do.

- We show the students the Lucky Charms cereal graph that we have drawn on a chart, which is shown on page 38. We explain that everyone will work together to complete the graph using one big bag of cereal. We ask the class to join us

This activity provides an opportunity for all students in the class, individually and as a group, to practice basic math skills. For the activity to be accomplished effectively, we assign certain jobs to specific students so that everyone gets a turn to help in the process. We assign the tasks according to the children's abilities to ensure the students' success with the project.

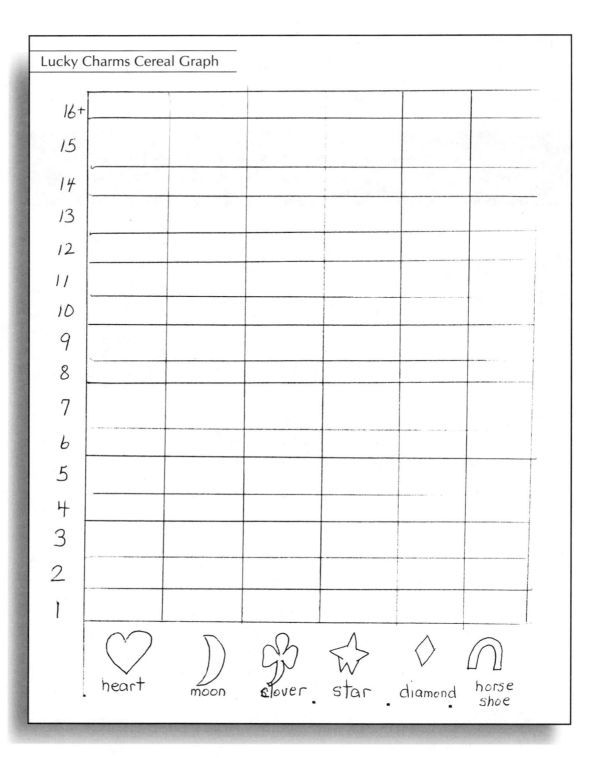

Lucky Charms Cereal Graph

on the carpet, with everyone sitting around the edge. We put a large piece of paper in the middle of the carpet for sorting and counting. We help the children sort the cereal into groups on the paper. They count how many shapes are in each group and color in the appropriate spaces on the chart to correspond to the sorting.

- We instruct the students to return to their seats and complete the activity individually with their own bags of cereal. I work with the ESOL students to make sure they understand the concepts of sorting, grouping, and counting.

ASSESSMENT

Assessment for this activity comes formally when we check to see if the students follow the directions in completing their own graphs.

Story Retelling

Retelling the story gives all students another chance to practice and develop oral language skills, with vocabulary that is now familiar. This activity is especially beneficial to the ESOL students because it provides them with an opportunity to practice oral language in a small, safe setting. The activity also serves as a culmination for the unit and helps bring unity and closure.

Goal 1, Standard 3   **To use English to communicate in social settings: Students will use learning strategies to extend their communicative competence.**

Descriptors

- practicing new language
- learning and using language "chunks"
- seeking support and feedback from others
- listening to and imitating how others use English

Progress Indicators

- recite a story aloud
- practice recently learned language
- test appropriate use of new vocabulary, phrases, and structures

---

Goal 2, Standard 3   **To use English to achieve academically in all content areas: Students will use appropriate learning strategies to construct and apply academic knowledge.**

Descriptors

- using context to construct meaning
- actively connecting new information to information previously learned
- imitating the behaviors of native English speakers to complete tasks successfully

Progress Indicators

- use pictures to check comprehension of a story
- rehearse and visualize information
- rephrase, explain, revise, and expand oral information to check comprehension

PROCEDURE

- First, we let the students color the Little Red Hen picture cards, which are shown below. Then they cut them out and put them in the correct sequence.

- Then we put the students into small groups and allow time for each member to retell the story to the small group. We mix the ESOL students in with the other students. This gives them a chance to hear and model language from the other students in their group. During this part

This activity allows the ESOL students a chance to practice their newly acquired language in a familiar environment. "The Little Red Hen" is a good story to use because of its repetitive story pattern.

Little Red Hen Picture Cards

Hen

duck

dog

cat

bread

of the activity, Jennifer and I walk around from group to group to listen to their versions of the story. I encourage the ESOL students to tell what they can of the story, helping them tell it at their level of language proficiency.

- After allowing sufficient time for sharing within the small groups, we ask the students to bring their colored picture cards and join us on the carpet for large-group time. We encourage the students to take turns joining in the retelling of the story for the large group. Our encouragement comes in a variety of forms to allow success for all students, no matter what their level of oral language proficiency is. Some students can retell the whole story on their own, or the teacher can read the story while the student shows the pictures, and there are variations in between these two. We adjust the task to meet the needs of our students.

ASSESSMENT

Assessment is conducted informally as we listen to each student retell the story. We listen to see if the students can name the characters in the story, tell the events that happened in the story, and say in what order these events took place.

Conclusion

This unit of study relating to the food groups provides an excellent opportunity to add an element of diversity to our teaching. It allows our ESOL students to share information from their own knowledge base to see how they are different, yet the same.

This unit is enjoyable for the students as well as educational and cross-cultural. I hope these ideas can be used as a springboard to help guide other teachers in the development of their own units. Things to consider in planning a unit include resources in the school, community resources available, personal knowledge base, and materials available. Be creative and have fun developing and teaching this unit of study.

RESOURCES AND REFERENCES

Children's Literature

During story or reading time, teachers could read one of the following stories to students. They could also have some of these stories recorded on audiotape to have available in a listening center.

Czernecki, S. (1992). *The sleeping bread.* Chicago: Hypertension.
  This book is a simple story about working in the kitchen to make bread with one's family.

Dooley, N. (1996). *Everybody bakes bread.* Minneapolis, MN: Carolihoda Books.
  A rainy day trip introduces Carrie to many different kinds of bread. Breads of many types are discussed.

Gershator, D., & Gershator, P. (1995). *Bread is for eating.* New York: Henry Holt.
  Mamita explains to her family how bread is made. The book includes a song in English and Spanish.

Harbison, E. (1997). *Loaves of fun: A history of bread.* Chicago: Chicago Review Press.
  This book uses a time line format to show the history of bread and includes recipes and activities.

Hoban, R. (1993). *Bread and jam for Frances.* New York: Scholastic.
  This is a charming story about trying to get a child to eat.

Morris, A. (1989). *Bread, bread, bread* (K. Heyman, Photographer). New York: Lothrop, Lee, & Shephard.
  This story introduces students to various types of bread from around the world.

Teacher Resources

Computer Curriculum Corporation. (1994). First adventures bookshelf [Computer software]. Sunnyvale, CA: Author.

Computer Curriculum Corporation. (1996). Discover English [Computer software]. Sunnyvale, CA: Author.

Kentucky Department of Education. (1999). *Transformations: Kentucky's curriculum framework.* Frankfort, KY: Author. (Available from Kentucky Department of Education, Division of Curriculum Development, 500 Mero Street, 18th floor, Frankfort, KY 40601)

McCloskey, M., Hooper, S., Linse, C., & Schottman, E. (1996). The little red hen. In *Amazing English! Teaching language, literature, and culture: An integrated ESL curriculum.* Reading, MA: Addison-Wesley.

TESOL. (1997). *ESL standards for pre-K–12 students.* Alexandria, VA: Author.

TESOL. (in press). *Scenarios for ESL standards-based assessment.* Alexandria, VA: Author.

UNIT 3
The World of Work: Choices and Opportunities

ESTHER RETISH

Introduction

> Angela was excited when she came to school this morning. She whispered, "My father is coming to talk to the ESL class this afternoon." We talked about how she would introduce him.
>
> That afternoon, Dr. George came to class to speak about his work as a psychiatrist. Angela introduced her dad and explained, "He helps sad people." Dr. George continued, "I do research on the brain and the severe depression caused by lesions on the brain."
>
> The students listened politely. Then Sarah leaned over to me and said, "Can he draw a picture?" I asked Dr. George to draw pictures to help the students understand, and he agreed. He drew the head and brain. He pointed to the picture and then his brain and explained, "Lesions are sores or hurts on the brain that make people so sad that they don't want to leave their houses." The students could then better understand what he was saying and ask questions. Three of the students concluded, "I want to do what Dr. George does when I grow up."

These teaching moments confirmed that students were engaged in the content of this unit and that it was appropriate for them at this stage in their English language development.

Context

Grade levels: First, second, and third grades, with adaptations for kindergarten

English proficiency level: Mixed beginning (absolute beginners to those with some English)

Native languages of students: Multilingual representation, including Spanish, Chinese, Arabic, Korean, and Japanese

Focus of instruction: Language development, social studies

Type of class: ESL pullout

Length of unit: 4 weeks (or as much time as you have)

Unit Overview

It is the third trimester of the year, and I am reflecting on the progress made by the students during this school year. There are a few students who need a boost to better reach their potential. Some of these students have been here only a few months, whereas others started at the beginning of the school year but have not taken off as expected. Although they had been in different pullout groups, I have put them together and developed this unit on work.

In the school where I teach, kindergarten and the first and second grades include a social studies unit on communities and people who live and work in these communities. Thus, this unit complements the mainstream kindergarten and first- and second-grade social studies curricula. I also want to reinforce previously presented vocabulary on home, family, and school. In this way, I am consciously preparing the students for success in the mainstream classroom.

My unit goals specify that the students will accomplish the following:

Content

- learn about people in the community, including the jobs they do and where they work
- learn about jobs of parents
- learn vocabulary associated with occupations

Language

- use reading strategies to decode and comprehend information that is read
- use the information learned in class to write about jobs
- use capital letters, periods, and noun-verb agreement in student writing

Learning Strategies

- evaluate their own preferences for work
- think about occupations that would be interesting when they themselves become adults
- involve their families in this unit
- invite their parents to share their expertise

This unit is divided into five parts:

1. Introduction: overview of the unit
2. Work at Home: jobs in the home and the people who perform them
3. Work at School: jobs at school and the people who perform them
4. Work of Parents: jobs of parents in and out of the home
5. Work in the Future: job possibilities for these students when they are adults

The unit overview on page 45 shows the activities for each part of the unit.

Standards

My goal for the students is for them to be able to communicate in all situations, not just in the ESL classroom. I am teaching a group of students who need a great deal of practice using English. I want to use some vocabulary they know and visit it in a new context. I want to be sure they complete the year knowing family, school, and home words.

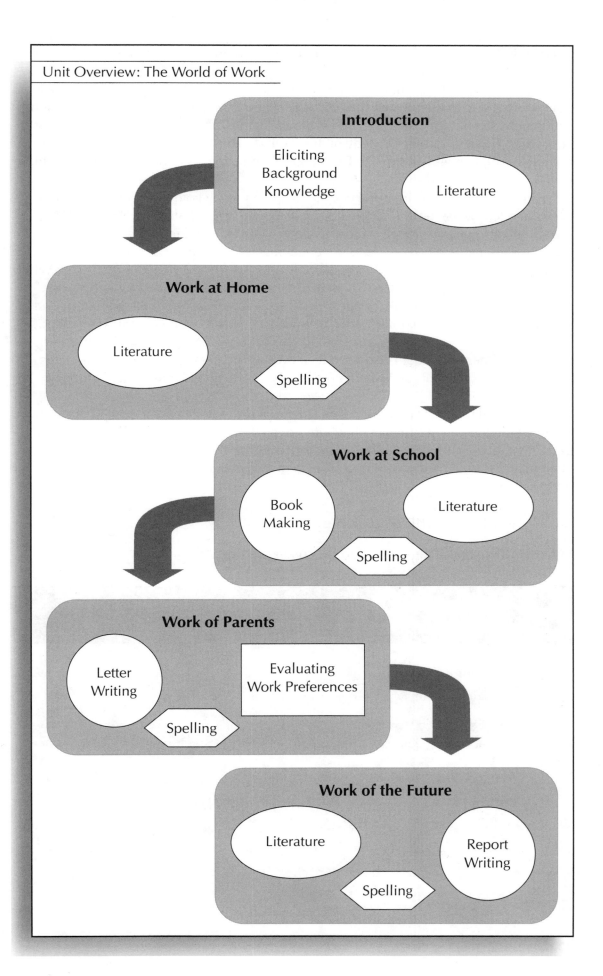

This ties in with the community theme in their classrooms and the home-school connection that our school promotes. I feel it is most important to include families in what we do at school. I send letters home to parents about what we are doing, call them, make a point of speaking to them when they come to school, and generally promote communication between the ESL classroom and students' homes. The other area that I am most concerned about is carryover. Many of my ESOL students speak a lot in my classroom but are fairly silent elsewhere. The ESL standards are a means to help achieve all of these goals.

With these thoughts in mind, I began my planning by going to my usual sources: books and fellow teachers. I read *ESL Standards for Pre-K–12 Students* (TESOL, 1997), especially the vignettes, to see if other teachers were teaching in similar ways. Each vignette demonstrates how students are encouraged to talk in class and share their thoughts and ideas. Then I read the standards upon which the vignettes are based. When I read the first descriptor for Goal 1, Standard 1, "sharing and requesting information" (p. 31) and the second sample progress indicator, "volunteer information and respond to questions about self and family" (p. 31), I said, "Yes, this is what I am thinking about." These standards also help with assessment, which I wrestle with often. I feel that I know where the students are, but I also need to show this progress to others. The standards also expand my thoughts and remind me of other areas that I know about but might forget.

After reading *ESL Standards*, I went to school the next day and talked to one of my favorite kindergarten teachers, with whom I often brainstorm ideas. This unit is based upon my thoughts, the ESL standards, brainstorming with other teachers, a previous attempt at this topic, and most important, the needs of the students who will be experiencing the unit.

Activities, Part I: Introduction

PURPOSE: TO INTRODUCE THE STUDENTS TO THE CONCEPT OF WORK.

Goal 2, Standard 1   To use English to achieve academically in all content areas: Students will use English to interact in the classroom.

Descriptors

- asking and answering questions
- participating in group discussions
- elaborating and extending other people's ideas and words

Progress Indicators

- respond appropriately to questions asked in class
- follow class discussions
- follow directions

Goal 2, Standard 3 To use English to achieve academically in all content areas: Students will use appropriate learning strategies to construct and apply academic knowledge.

Descriptors

- focusing attention selectively
- actively connecting new information to information previously learned
- recognizing the need for and seeking assistance appropriately from others

Progress Indicators

- explain, pantomime, and draw pictures for work vocabulary to help peers and to demonstrate understanding of the vocabulary
- use appropriate vocabulary during discussion and interaction with peers
- follow directions demonstrated by pictures drawn for class activity

Eliciting Background Knowledge

PROCEDURE

- I tell the students we are beginning a new unit. I ask them if they know what the word *work* means. I ask questions such as

    Do your parents work?

    What work do they do?

    Where do they work?

    Why do people work?

    Does everybody work?

    Do you work?

- I record this information on a chart labeled "What We Know About Work." At intervals during the unit we return to the chart to confirm our knowledge and to ad to it. The chart hangs where stude can refer to it for ideas and for spelling.

KINDERGARTEN ADAPTATION

I ask students to draw the work their pare do. Then I ask them to draw work they d discuss the differences and similarities.

Asking the students questions about the topic gives me information about where we are beginning. It guides me in the vocabulary I can use and demonstrates the experiences students have had with the concept of work.

I feel that each class should contain some English that the students know, some that they do not know, and some that I am evaluating. Thus, each class helps the students realize that they are learning a lot of English, but that they also have more to learn. This also helps me plan appropriate lessons on areas needing more work.

- Parent/Family Involvement: I send a note home to parents explaining what we discuss during this unit. I include a general overview of the topic, the targeted vocabulary words, and areas for parent involvement. I want the parents to know that they will be asked to speak to the class about their work in about 2 weeks.

Literature: *I'm Too Small. You're Too Big*

PROCEDURE

- The book *I'm Too Small. You're Too Big* (Barrett, 1981) is simply written and has self-explanatory pictures to help students follow the concept. It is also entertaining and silly, which helps students who are struggling with English.

- After reading the book aloud to students, I talk with the students about appropriate behaviors in the home. For example, the father is riding a tricycle for which he is obviously too big, while the son is driving a car, which he is too small to do. The students give examples of activities they are too small to do and the opposite for their parents.

- I divide the class into two groups, telling one group to draw pictures of things they can do but their parents are too big to do. I tell the other group to draw pictures of activities their parents can do but they are too small to do. Another option is to have all students draw two pictures, one of things their parents are too big to do and the other of things they are too small to do.

- I write on the chalkboard: *I'm too small to . . . and My mom/dad is too big to . . . .* I tell the students to write these words on their papers and finish the sentences (e.g., *I'm too small to sit at my dad's desk and chair at work. My dad is too big to sit in my chair and desk at school.*).

- After students finish, I collect the pictures and match the ones that go together, saying the phrase, "I'm too small to . . . , but my parents are too big to . . . ." If there are pictures without a match, I ask students to brainstorm ideas and to draw these extra pictures. I put the pictures in a pocket chart with the phrase below it (e.g., *I'm too small to drive the car, but you're too big to ride my bike.*). (See sample student pictures on p. 49.)

- Parent/Family Involvement: We practice reading these phrases, and then I bind them into a class book. I let the students take the book home for one night to read to their parents. We add a comment page to the end of the book, and I ask the students to have their parents write a comment in our book. Each day when the book comes back, we read the comments written by parents.

ASSESSMENT

Throughout the class, I observe the students to determine who is responding, following class discussion, following directions, drawing appropriate pictures, writing on each picture, and completing assignments during class time.

I have a small notebook with tabs for each student. I write notes about the students in this notebook as I observe them during class. I try to transfer this information onto the school district Student Proficiency Profile on a regular basis.

Activities, Part 2: Work at Home

PURPOSE: TO NAME THE JOBS AT HOME AND THE PEOPLE WHO PERFORM THEM, AND TO PRACTICE HOME VOCABULARY IN CONTEXT.

Goal 1, Standard 2 **To use English to communicate in social settings: Students will interact in, through, and with spoken and written English for personal expression and enjoyment.**

Descriptors

- describing, reading about, or participating in a favorite activity
- sharing social and cultural traditions and values
- expressing personal needs, feelings, and ideas

Progress Indicators

- respond appropriately to a book
- describe a favorite character in a book
- use vocabulary to talk about a work activity at home
- ask information questions
- describe activities at home

Literature: *I Love My Family*

PROCEDURE

- I like to teach with books. As I read *I Love My Family* (Beal, 1991), I ask the students: "Does your father live in your house? Does your mother live in your house?" In this way, we name the people in the book and compare them to the people in students' homes. We go back through the book and talk about what these people do in their homes. We then discuss what the students do in their homes. We talk about responsibility and what they can do at home to help. One student mentions something to remind others that they do the same things, such as wash dishes or set the table. This is a perfect time to introduce idiomatic expressions such as *make the bed* or *do the dishes.*

- We make a chart of the people in the students' homes and the work they do there.

- After we talk about the people in their homes, I tell the students: "Draw a picture of yourself and a person in your house doing something together. If you can, write what you are doing on the picture." When the pictures are completed, we talk about the ways students work with their families at home.

- I handle student writing in many ways. Students can use invented spelling while they are writing, and this can be corrected later. Words used by many students can be written on the chalkboard. A word wall can be developed with this unit so students can refer to these words as needed. Peers can spell for each other. The teacher can walk around and spell for students as requested or needed. Picture dictionaries can also be used. The "What We Know About Work" chart and the chart on people in the home and jobs they do are displayed as another source for spelling words needed by students.

Spelling Words

Spelling is taught the same way in each part of the unit.

PROCEDURE

- After making the chart in the previous activity, we look at the words most often used. These become the spelling words for Part 2.

Spelling Words

home	wash
mom	shop
dad	make the bed
cook	set the table
clean	do the dishes

- Each week I give the students vocabulary words as spelling words. We talk about the meaning of each word and use it in several sentences. I read the words one at a time, use them in sentences, and then the students spell them as best they can. At the end, I write the words on the chalkboard. The students correct their words and rewrite them the corrected way. I then check their lists to make sure all the words they are studying for the week are spelled correctly. This gives me a chance to evaluate students' letter/sound associations, the basic collection of words they can spell, and note their handwriting ability. I tell the students that the emphasis is on how they spell on the final test and if they can spell these words correctly when they use them in their writing.

Literature: *Piggybook*

PROCEDURE

- I tell the students, "I am going to read you a most unusual book, entitled *Piggybook* (Browne, 1986), about how people feel about working at home. Look very closely at the pictures. You will begin to see pigs in the pictures. Pigs lie in mud to cool off. This leads some people to say pigs are dirty. Look at the pictures. Is the house getting dirtier or messier? How do you think the father and sons feel living in a dirty house? Where do you think the mother went?" Later in the book, when the mother comes home, I ask, "How do the father and sons feel? What do they promise to do? What does the mother want to do, and why?" This book also tells us about responsibility. I ask students, "How do you feel when no one helps you pick up your toys and you have to do it all by yourself, even if you did not make the mess? How do your parents feel about setting the table, making everyone's bed, and washing the dishes by themselves? What can you do to help at home?"

- I tell the students, "You are going to make a book about the people in your home and what they do, including you." I give each of them a folder with four sheets of white paper and say, "On each page, I want you to draw a picture of your mother working at home." We share ideas about what to draw, such as cooking food, washing clothes, and cleaning the house. I tell them, "After you draw the picture, write a sentence telling what your mom is doing, for example, 'My mother cooks Korean food.'" If the students need more paper, they are given more, but giving them four sheets encourages them to draw at least four pictures. The students put their names on the folders and keep their papers inside them.

- We continue this activity in the next class, when students draw pictures of other people working at home: their fathers, siblings, grandparents, or anyone else who lives in the home. I encourage the students to label their pictures with words, phrases, or sentences, depending on their level. This provides practice using the vocabulary words in context, spelling the words, and writing phrases or sentences.

Sometimes the students do not live with both parents, so they draw whoever lives in their home and performs the different jobs. We talk about how interesting it is that different people live in different family structures.

- After the pictures are complete, we review the parts of a book: title page, author, publisher, place, and date. The students write title pages for their books, list themselves as authors, write "Published in the ESL room at Roosevelt School," and include the date. I then bind the books, and the students can take them home. However, they must show their books to their classroom teachers and friends before taking them home. This encourages the ESOL students to talk to their peers and teachers.

KINDERGARTEN ADAPTATION

I also read these books to the kindergartners. I tell them, "Draw a picture of each person in your home at work and write what each person is doing on your picture." I write what they "read" to me in standard English so their families will know what they wrote, in case they forget. I ask the students to write a title, to write their names as authors, and to include Iowa City and the year. Then I bind the books and ask students to show them to their teachers and friends before taking them home.

ASSESSMENT

I evaluate how the students respond in class discussions: the appropriateness, vocabulary, and grammar used. This helps me determine what areas need more practice. I may do a minilesson on using *I* instead of *me* to begin a sentence, use of plurals when talking about more than one, or noun-verb agreement.

I evaluate the pictures students draw for appropriateness and developmental level. I also evaluate the words written under the pictures for letter-sound associations, appropriateness, vocabulary, and grammatical structures. Again, I may do a minilesson reminding students to begin a sentence with a capital letter and to end it with a period.

I use my anecdotal notebook and our Student Proficiency Profile to record each student's level of expertise.

Activities, Part 3: Work at School

PURPOSE: TO DISCUSS, ASK QUESTIONS, AND WRITE ABOUT A FAMILIAR TOPIC WITH APPROPRIATE VOCABULARY.

Goal 2, Standard 2 To use English to achieve academically in all content areas: Students will use English to obtain, process, construct, and provide subject matter information in spoken and written form.

Descriptors

- gathering information orally and in writing
- retelling information
- representing information visually and interpreting information presented visually

Progress Indicators

- describe work done by different people at school
- use appropriate names for school jobs
- predict what work school people do
- ask school people about the work they do
- choose school people to interview
- write what was learned from the interview
- use appropriate grammatical structures and spelling orally and in written form

Book Making

PROCEDURE

- I tell the students that I looked for a book about people who work at school in our library but could not find one, and I suggest that we write our own. (I later find one in the University Curriculum Library. After we complete our book, I read it to the students and we decide to keep our book the way it is.)

- I say to students, "We have been talking about the work people do. This time we are going to talk about people at school. Who are the people who work at this school?" We generate a long list of the people who work at our school, and I write their jobs on a large sheet of paper. We go back over the list and talk about what each person does. I write key words next to each job.

- I tell the students, "This is the time to choose the person or job you want to write about. Each person has one choice. If two people choose the same job, you can work together." We then talk about what to include in this description. I tell them, "Observe your person working at school and ask the person questions about the job. Each job will be a chapter in our book, and you can write as many pages as you want. I will type the information, and you can illustrate the pages."

- I read what each student has written and offer editing suggestions. The students rewrite and then give their papers to me to type. I type what they have written into Easy Book Deluxe (Rappoport, 1997). This is a computer program that prints text on both sides of the page so that the printout looks like a real book. The students reread their writing on the computer screen before printing the final copy. After the chapter is printed, the students illustrate the pages they have written.

- Students then choose another school worker. They can either continue to work with the same peers or change. We continue until every job on the list we made has been written about and illustrated.

- I make a copy of each chapter for the students who wrote it. Students who finish before others can illustrate their copies to take home or read them to peers and school workers.

- We bind the books with a small stick or twig and a rubber band. We punch two holes in the paper, like a two-ring notebook, thread a rubber band end through each hole, and attach it to the twig. The students take their books home.

- The original chapters become a class book. We vote on a title; write a table of contents; alphabetize students' names; design a title page; and establish the publisher, location, and date (sample pages shown on pp. 55–56). We also add a page at the end for comments.

- Parent/Family Involvement: The 123-page bound book goes home with a different student each night (by alphabetical order), and the parents are asked to write about how they like the book on the comment page. Parent comments are read at the beginning of the next class.

KINDERGARTEN ADAPTATION

Kindergartners write about what their teachers do in the kindergarten and what they do. They dictate this to me and I type it into Easy Book Deluxe. We then read and discuss each page and illustrate it appropriately. These books go home to be shared with the students' families.

ASSESSMENT

I make notes about the progress of students in my anecdotal notebook. I also use our school district's Student Proficiency Profile to follow their developmental levels.

A third- and fourth-grade teacher in our school does several plays with her students each year, so I decided to try a play with the kindergarten group using the theme of people at school.

For example:

Tony (as teacher): Good morning, Jun Suk. Good morning, Sarah. Good morning, Sasha. Hang up your school bags and come into the room.

Students: Good morning, teacher.

Students enter the classroom and say good morning to each other.

I recommend including only a few activities in the play, such as show-and-tell, lining up, and journal writing, and having only one or two students act as teacher rather than all the students. This, plus discussion, is probably enough material for the play.

Roosevelt School
Workers

by

E.S.L. Students at
Roosevelt

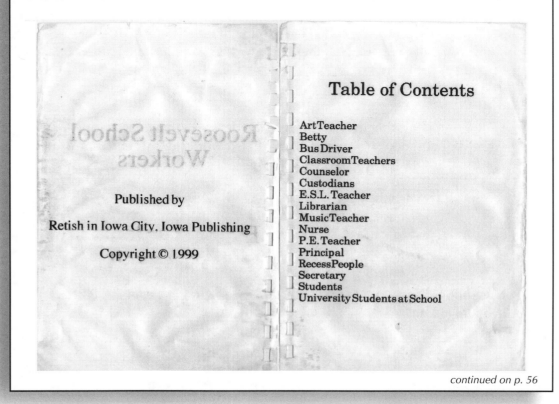

Published by

Retish in Iowa City, Iowa Publishing

Copyright © 1999

Table of Contents

continued on p. 56

Teachers like to eat snacks with their students.

8

Teachers talk to students.

9

I evaluate (a) the description of work done by the people who work at school and the appropriate use of names for these jobs; (b) the use of correct spelling of core words from the spelling lists; (c) the content, clarity, and grammatical structures in the writing; and (d) students' ability to read what they have written and illustrate it appropriately.

Spelling Words

PROCEDURE

- I tell the students that these words are the ones most often used for people who work at school. These are their spelling words for this part of the unit:

Spelling Words

teacher	writing
music	talking
art	run
math	play ball
reading	

- Suggestions for how to teach spelling can be found in Activities, Part 2: Work at Home (see p. 51).

Activities, Part 4: Work of Parents

PURPOSE: TO INVOLVE PARENTS IN OUR DISCUSSION ON WORK, SHARE PARENTS' EXPERTISE, AND INCREASE WORK VOCABULARY WORDS TO INCLUDE PARENTS' JOBS.

Goal 2, Standard 2 To use English to achieve academically in all content areas: Students will use English to obtain, process, construct, and provide subject matter information in spoken and written form.

Descriptors

- listening to, speaking, reading, and writing about subject matter information
- gathering information orally and in writing
- retelling information
- formulating and asking questions

Progress Indicators

- edit and revise own written assignments
- generate and ask questions of adults about their work
- record observations about work preferences

Goal 3, Standard 1 To use English in socially and culturally appropriate ways: Students will use the appropriate language variety, register, and genre according to audience, purpose, and setting.

Descriptors

- using the appropriate degree of formality with different audiences and settings
- recognizing and using standard English and vernacular dialects appropriately
- determining appropriate topics for interaction
- using a variety of writing styles appropriate for different audiences, purposes, and settings

Progress Indicators

- write a letter to an adult family member using appropriate language forms
- introduce parents to the class
- interact with an adult in a formal setting

Letter Writing
PROCEDURE

- We have talked about the people who work at school. Now we talk about other jobs people do. I ask the students what their parents do. Some students mention that their parents are teachers, work in a hospital, or stay home and take care of them. Others know that their parents go to the university or go to work someplace. I suggest we ask their parents to come to school to tell us about the work they are doing here or the work they did in their native countries.

- This is an appropriate time for a minilesson on letter writing. I talk about the kinds of letters one can write and to whom. The emphasis in this first minilesson is on invitations. I discuss the idea that letters to parents are not as formal as some others, but good sentences are still important. I discuss the closing for a letter to a family member versus the *sincerely* that we usually use.

- Parent/Family Involvement: Students write letters home inviting their parents to come to class to speak to us about their work. We discuss appropriate behavior during parent presentations, such as raising hands to speak and waiting to be called upon, and we discuss the kinds of questions to ask. We also practice introducing parents and briefly saying what the parent does.

  It is very helpful for the teacher to send a note home along with the letters of invitation asking parents to indicate a preferred date and time to come and speak. Scheduling their presentations will help avoid having too many parents show up unexpectedly at the same time and will thus allow ample time for each presenter.

- After the parent's presentations, students write letters to each of the speakers, thanking them and noting an interesting idea they learned from each one. I put two phrases on the board for those who need them: *Thank you for talking to us about . . .* and *I learned that . . . .* I remind them of the difference between signing a letter to their own parents and signing a thank-you note to someone else's.

Spelling Words
PROCEDURE

- I give the students spelling words that they need for letter writing:

Spelling Words

job	interesting
work	dear
talking	sincerely
liked	thank you

- Suggestions for how to teach spelling can be found in Activities, Part 2: Work at Home (see p. 51).

Evaluating Work Preferences

This activity on choices people make when deciding on a career can be used either in this part of the unit or the next. I used it here to help students think about their parents' work and to stimulate questions to ask the parents.

PROCEDURE

- We talk about the ideas in the book *People Working* (Florian, 1983), and then I read it to them. I give each student a blank piece of paper on which to create a questionnaire, telling them, "Write your name in the top left corner, the date in the top right corner, and the numbers 1 to 10 down the left-hand side of the paper."

- I read the following questions about work preferences to the students. I also read the key words that I put on the chalkboard after each question so students can respond more accurately. (Key words on the chalkboard are noted in parentheses below.) I give several examples of jobs in each area to help the students understand the questions. I also use the book as a visual representation of the questions. The questionnaire helps reinforce ideas from the book.

  1. Do you want to work with other people or by yourself? (others/alone)
  2. Do you want to work during the day or at night? (day/night)
  3. Do you want to make a lot of money or just a little? (a lot/a little)
  4. Do you want to work with people, as teachers, doctors, and dentists do? (people/no people)
  5. Do you want to work outdoors or inside? (outdoors/inside)
  6. Do you want to work with animals? (animals/no animals)
  7. Do you want to move around a lot or sit in a chair much of the time? (move/sit)
  8. Do want to go to school many years to learn your job or go just a few years? (many/a few)
  9. Do you like mathematics, science, reading, writing, history, music, art? (write all subjects on the chalkboard)
  10. Do you want to work many hours or a few? (many/a few)

- We use the questionnaire to discuss the jobs the parents present, comparing and contrasting the requirements of each.

KINDERGARTEN ADAPTATION

Kindergartners invite their parents to speak to their class. Letters of invitation and thank-you notes are written together. We discuss the differences between the two. The book on work is read, but no questionnaire is given. We discuss the ideas together.

ASSESSMENT

To assess students, I do the following: (a) observe the behavior of the students with the speakers, (b) listen for grammatically correct sentence structure in questions, (c) listen for the content in the sentences, (d) listen for comprehension orally and in reading, and (e) look at writing ability in sentence structure and content.

I also make notes on these areas in my anecdotal notebook and note progress on our district Student Proficiency Profile.

Activities, Part 5: Work of the Future

PURPOSE: TO IDENTIFY JOBS OF INTEREST TO THE STUDENTS AND LEARN ABOUT THESE JOBS.

Goal 2, Standard 2   To use English to achieve academically in all content areas: Students will use English to obtain, process, construct, and provide subject matter information in spoken and written form.

Descriptors

- comparing and contrasting information
- listening to, speaking, and writing about subject matter information
- gathering information orally and in writing
- responding to the work of peers and others
- demonstrating knowledge through application in a variety of contexts

Progress Indicators

- interview school workers about their jobs
- locate reference material
- gather and organize the appropriate materials needed to complete a task
- edit and revise own and peers' written assignments

Spelling Words

PROCEDURE

- The spelling words for this part of the unit include vocabulary students will need to write their reports about jobs that interest them.

Spelling Words

money	inside
people	outside
school	years
day	hours
night	

- Suggestions for how to teach spelling can be found in Activities, Part 2: Work at Home (see p. 51).

Report Writing

PROCEDURE

- To get the process started, the students look at books, write interview questions, and use the classroom computer to search the Internet for information about occupations of interest. I start each class by reading and discussing a book and reviewing the information students are learning on their own. They work either individually or in groups; I walk around the room talking to students about what they are learning and helping them write the information. The following books are used during this discovery period:

> *When We Grow Up* (Rockwell, 1981)
>
> *100 Words About Working* (Brown, 1988)
>
> *Mommies at Work* (Merriam, 1989)
>
> *My Daddy Is a Nurse* (Wando & Blank, 1981)
>
> *People at Work* (Perham, 1986)

- I remind students, "Remember the questions you answered about work. For example, would you prefer working during the day or night, going to school for a few years or many years, working with people or not? Think about what you want when you look at job possibilities."

- As the students think of possible jobs, we take out books from the library on these areas. We also search the Internet for additional information.

- Parent/Family Involvement: Students ask their parents for information about the jobs they are researching. Many choose the same profession as their parents, so their parents can provide more information about the job.

- I give students a worksheet with questions on it to guide their writing. They can write by themselves or in groups about the job they would like to do. Before they write, I discuss my job as an ESL teacher as an example:

  1. Job: ESL teacher

  2. What do you do for this job? *I teach English to students who do not know English.*

  3. When do you do this job? *I work during the day from 8:00 a.m. to 4:00 p.m.*

  4. How do you get to do this job? *I had to go to the university to learn how to teach students.*

  5. Why do you want to do this job? *I get to work with very interesting students.*

A copy of the job information worksheet is shown on page 62.

- As students read their reports, I videotape them. We watch these presentations, evaluate them, point out the good things, and revise the speeches. I then videotape the revised presentations, and we show these videos to families at our end-of-the-year gathering.

The jobs this class chose were in the following professions: medical, teaching, piloting, and firefighting. With more time, I would have invited guest speakers to talk about several of the jobs that students had expressed interest in. We would listen to people who actually do the jobs talk about them and ask questions we had developed ahead of time. Then the students would choose an area based upon hearing about many different options.

```
Job Information Worksheet

Name: _____

Date: _____

1. Job: _____

2. What do you do for this job?

3. When do you do this job?

4. How do you get to do this job?

5. Why do you want to do this job?
```

KINDERGARTEN ADAPTATION

I choose a few occupations to teach the kindergartners that follow their kindergarten curriculum. We learn about farmers, doctors, nurses, police officers, and firefighters. When we finish, the students choose their favorite occupations and draw themselves as that person.

ASSESSMENT

I make notes on the following areas in my anecdotal notebook and indicate progress on our district Student Proficiency Profile: (a) grammatical structures in oral and written language, (b) ability to work with peers, (c) ability to edit what was written, (d) content of reports written, (e) ability to present material orally, and (f) ability to take information learned and put it into a report.

Each time I come to the assessment aspect of this unit, I struggle with what to use, how to write it up, how to make it consistent, and how to go about it efficiently. I keep returning to the unit objectives and progress indicators, and find myself building an assessment rubric, adding more ideas. The rubric shown on page 63 is a work in progress.

RESOURCES AND REFERENCES

Children's Literature

Canizares, S., & Chessen, B. (1999). *Jobs*. New York: Scholastic.
   The photographs of people at work are accompanied by simple text.

Barrett, J. (1981). *I'm too small. You're too big*. New York: Antheneum.
   Text and pictures contrast the size differences between father and son.

Beal, K. (1991). *I love my family*. Reading, MA: Addison-Wesley.
   Each page shows a family member and child in an activity.

| Rubric |

Student Name: _____ Date _____

Unit Goals	Not Yet	Inconsistent	Consistent
Content			
Identifies people in community			
Describes jobs and work that people in community do			
Describes jobs and work parents do			
Identifies school workers			
Describes jobs and work that school workers do			
Uses vocabulary associated with jobs			
Language			
Follows class discussions			
Follows directions			
Uses target vocabulary			
Asks questions for clarification			
Asks questions for information			
Uses information learned to respond in class			
Uses information learned to write about jobs			
Uses reading strategies to decode			
Uses reading strategies for comprehension			
Uses capital letters and periods appropriately			
Uses noun-verb agreement appropriately			
Uses word order appropriately			
Learning Strategies			
Has a logical rationale for job preference			
Shows evidence of family involvement (for teacher information)			
Uses auditory learning style			
Uses kinesthetic learning style			
Uses visual learning style			

Berger, S., & Chanko, P. (1999). *School.* New York: Scholastic.
This book includes photographs and simple text about people who work in school.

Brown, R. (Illustrator). (1988). *100 words about working.* Orlando, FL: Harcourt Brace Jovanovich.
This book includes labeled illustrations of 100 different types of work that people do.

Browne, M. (1986). *Piggybook.* New York: Alfred A. Knopf.
When mother unexpectedly leaves one day, her demanding family begins to realize just how much she does for them.

Burton, M., French, C., & Jones, T. (1999). *Working together.* Pelham, NY: Benchmark Education.
Working Together *includes pictures and simple text of children working at home with parents.*

Callahan, C., & Ossips, K. (Eds.). (1996). *My world.* Upper Saddle River, NJ: Prentice Hall Regents.
This book includes many cartoon-format illustrations of children and families working together.

Florian, D. (1983). *People working.* New York: Thomas Y. Crowell.
This book briefly describes where and how people work.

Johnson, J. (1987). *Teachers from A to Z.* New York: Walker.
The letters of the alphabet introduce aspects of elementary teachers' work lives, beginning with alphabet, books, chalkboard, desk, *and* education, *and continuing through the alphabet.*

Johnson, N. (1989). *All in a day's work.* Boston: Little, Brown.
Twelve Americans talk about their jobs, including a teacher, nurse, farmer, musician, pilot, assembly line worker, and judge.

LeSieg, T. (1980). *Maybe you should fly a jet! Maybe you should be a vet!* New York: Random House.
The rhymes in the book suggest a variety of occupational choices.

Merriam, E. (1989). *Mommies at work.* New York: Simon & Shuster.
This book examines many different jobs performed by working mothers, including counting money in banks and building bridges.

Perham, M. (1986). *People at work.* Minneapolis, MN: Dillion Press.
Text and photographs describe various jobs performed by people around the world, including nursing, fishing, sheep farming, film making, and fire fighting.

Rockwell, A. (1981). *When we grow up.* New York: E. P. Dutton.
Pictures and simple text illustrate the various jobs children want to have when they grow up.

Wando, M., & Blank, J. (1981). *My daddy is a nurse.* Reading, MA: Addison- Wesley.
This book describes the work of men with 10 occupations traditionally reserved for women, including nurse, flight attendant, homemaker, dental hygienist, librarian, and preschool teacher.

Teacher Resources

Rappoport, E. (1997). Easy book deluxe [Computer software]. Pleasantville, NY: Sunburst Communications.

TESOL. (1997). *ESL standards for pre-K–12 students.* Alexandria, VA: Author.

UNIT 4
"Eggs"citing Animals

JUDIE HAYNES *and* JUDITH B. O'LOUGHLIN

Introduction

Eight first- and second-grade ESOL students are sitting around a table looking at a variety of nonfiction picture books, which are open to show pictures and photographs of baby animals hatching from eggs. Questions about the animals and their eggs help students focus their observations. The conversation continues about the various animals in the pictures. We encourage one student to show us a picture of a snake. We then point to a picture of the mother duck and duckling and ask another student, "What is the baby duck called?" We ask a third student to describe what is happening in a picture of an egg hatching. As this student describes what the baby animals in the eggs are doing, we introduce the word hatched.

Through carefully planned questions asked at different levels of difficulty, we can accommodate the learning needs of all the students in this multilevel ESL group.

Context

Grade levels: Grades 1 and 2

English proficiency levels: Advanced beginning through intermediate

Native languages of students: Arabic, Gujarati, Japanese, Korean, Mandarin, Russian

Focus of instruction: Cross-content language development (e.g., science, literature, mathematics)

Type of class: Pullout, 30 minutes daily

Length of unit: 4 weeks

Most ESL teachers find that their biggest challenge is teaching a multiage, multilevel group of students. Although it is educationally logical to cluster Grades 1 and 2 together, there are often significant developmental differences between these two groups of students. We know that not everyone has the same understanding of the material. For example, second graders read and write more proficiently and with more depth of understanding than first graders. First graders are usually unable to read or work without teacher-directed and teacher-monitored activities, whereas second graders can often read and work somewhat independently. Also, the work that advanced beginning-level students produce is different from that of intermediate-level students. As we move through this unit, the age and ability levels of the students in the group help us decide which materials to select.

We are both ESL teachers in different districts of northern New Jersey. This unit and its activities represent a synthesis of our different practices. However, they are presented here as though they were being taught to one group of students in a single ESL class. These eight students represent a cross-section of our two student populations.

In our low-incidence districts, reading instruction is usually conducted by the first- or second-grade teacher in the mainstream classroom. As the ESL teachers, we support and reinforce classroom instruction by developing activities that help students gain extra practice with language. As is typical of ESL in low-incidence settings, our instruction is generally conducted in a 30- to 45-minute pullout session. The role of the ESL teacher, the instruction, and assessment all differ from those of schools with larger ESL populations.

As ESL teachers, we sometimes work separately from, and at other times parallel to, the mainstream classroom curriculum. The instruction reinforces classroom language arts instruction and reflects the same practices. The content does not necessarily mirror classroom units of study, but may elaborate and extend instructional units to help ESOL students increase their English language knowledge base. Instructional units such as "'Egg'citing Animals" are based on language arts activities, but also focus on science, social studies, health, and mathematics.

Unit Overview

The opening classroom scenario is part of the introduction to a 4-week unit on animals that hatch from eggs. The unit explores, extends, and expands students' general knowledge base of animals and helps them learn to see differences and make comparisons among various animals that hatch from eggs. Our unit on "'Eggs'citing Animals" is taught through a variety of learning modalities: visual, auditory, and kinesthetic. If the same students are in our class for several years, the unit can be repeated using different animals. For example, kindergartners may do a frog unit while first and second graders study birds and third graders study insects. This allows us to use some of the same materials and overlap some of the activities.

Our lessons throughout this unit facilitate student practice with a variety of vocabulary and concepts from content areas:

1. using color, number, and shape words

2. discriminating between fact and fiction, real and make-believe

3. developing appropriate adjectives to describe nouns

4. describing placement with prepositions

Certain language structures are introduced in the first grade and reinforced and refined in second-grade instruction. Therefore, we have embedded the following basic grammatical structures into our lessons:

1. present tense declarative statements
2. negative constructions using contractions
3. interrogative constructions, including yes/no and *wh-* questions
4. comparative and superlative forms of adjectives
5. prepositional phrases

Classroom language arts instruction includes language and vocabulary from other disciplines, such as science and mathematics, so we include counting words and appropriate scientific vocabulary in our unit.

We also develop goals for the unit overall: Students will

Content

- identify animals that hatch from eggs
- describe and differentiate the characteristics of various types of eggs
- identify and describe developmental changes in animals from egg to birth
- compare and contrast different pieces of literature related to the topic
- conduct science experiments using eggs and report the results

Language

- survey peers about their favorite kinds of eggs and graph the results
- read and discuss fiction and nonfiction related to the unit theme
- increase vocabulary through daily minilessons related to the unit theme
- learn idiomatic phrases
- increase oral narrative ability through daily debriefing activities

Learning Strategies

- play games and sing songs related to the unit theme to develop alternative learning modalities
- create art projects and models to explore alternative learning styles and nonverbal responses to content learning
- use a variety of writing activities (e.g., reporting results, describing processes and cycles, creating riddles and stories, comparing and contrasting information) in writing narratives

The unit overview on page 68 shows the planning web used in developing this unit.

Standards

Even before TESOL published *ESL Standards for Pre-K–12 Students* (TESOL, 1997), we focused on content-based ESL instruction. We knew that teaching English language skills through meaningful content activities would produce more competent language learners than teaching language skills in isolation. Our focus was to develop the whole child, not to teach islands of linguistic knowledge, so ESOL students could participate in mainstream classroom activities. We also knew from experience that the parents of our ESOL

Unit Overview: "Eggs"citing Animals

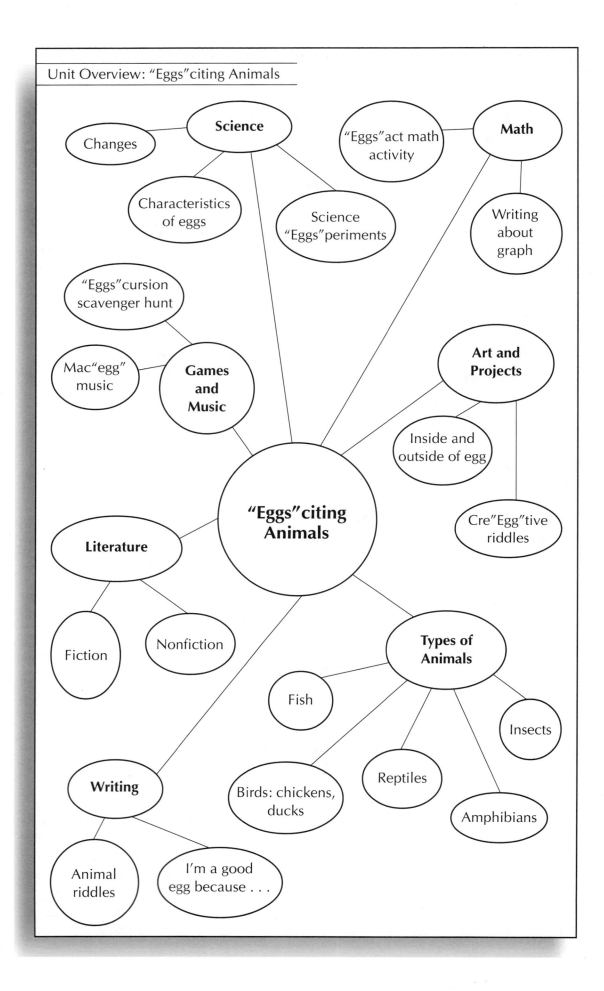

students saw the importance and value of our pullout instruction when it focused on learning English through content studies. Therefore, from the ESL standards, our focus had initially been on Goal 2, Standard 2: To use English to achieve academically in all content areas.

As we began to use the standards more, we found validation of our instructional objectives and activities in the content descriptors and discovered new ways to focus on content instruction by reviewing Goal 2 descriptors when we began a new unit.

We also discovered that many of the descriptors in Goal 1 (to use English to communicate in social settings) were intuitively included in all of our content instruction. In addition, the descriptors and sample progress indicators helped us develop narratives for **portfolio assessment** and parent conference checklists.

When we focused on the implications for instruction in Goal 3 (to use English in socially and culturally appropriate ways), we realized the importance of integrating Goal 3 descriptors into instruction. Learning to speak English and learning content in English are ultimately the main purposes of our instruction. However, delivery and demonstration of knowledge on the part of our students is not complete if they are unable to deliver their messages in socially and culturally appropriate ways. As teachers and models of appropriate language variations, we have to design activities that model and, in some instances, directly teach language appropriate for the task. Therefore, when students demonstrate what they have learned through oral presentations, class participation, or cooperative learning group activities, they show that they can do it in socially appropriate language (e.g., correct register, tone, volume, and language variety).

All our units use **performance-based assessment**. Students are assessed through oral retelling, round robin questioning (as described in the "Animal 'Eggs'amination" introductory lesson and the "Good Egg" idiom activity), writing projects, and other samples of their oral or written work. We feel that this type of assessment is appropriate to the students' grade and proficiency levels.

Our assessments are linguistically age appropriate, but less formal than traditional tests. For example, daily assessments often include a **debriefing** activity. In this type of activity, students must answer a question about the day's lesson in order to leave the ESL classroom and return to their regular classroom. Students who respond correctly the first time may leave. Students who cannot answer a question the first time get a second opportunity to answer a new question. All students are informally assessed in academic content (e.g., by having them recall, retell, and narrate) and sociocultural competence. In this way, we are aligning our assessment to Goals 2 and 3 of the ESL standards.

Students are also informally assessed in other oral activities, such as their ability to work with peers, respond to teacher questions, and communicate with other students. Class and group brainstorming activities and listening to, responding, repeating, or reflecting upon the responses of others are critical academic and culturally appropriate learning strategies used in U.S. elementary classrooms. These kinds of assessments connect with Goals 1 and 3 of the ESL standards.

Our units always include a cumulative assessment, which might be a writing activity, an art project, or a game. For example, in "Cre'Egg'tive Riddles," we combine creative thinking, recall, writing, and art. In this way, holistic student learning can be assessed without the stress related to the typical pencil-and-paper test.

Activities

Animal "Eggs"amination: Brainstorming and Shared Reading

In this activity, our students are learning how to listen to a story and appropriately join in a group discussion. As students brainstorm what they already know about eggs, they practice listening to each other and expand on their classmates' ideas. Although our group chart serves the same purpose as a K-W-L chart, we find that brainstorming for a typical K-W-L chart does not usually produce satisfactory results at this grade level with ESOL students.

Goal 2, Standard 2 To use English to achieve academically in all content areas: Students will use English to obtain, process, construct, and provide subject matter information in spoken and written form.

Descriptors

- hypothesizing
- gathering information orally
- retelling information
- listening to, speaking, reading, and writing about subject matter information

Progress Indicators

- construct a chart showing data
- classify objects
- show comprehension of a story read aloud
- record observations

Goal 3, Standard 1 To use English in socially and culturally appropriate ways: Students will use the appropriate language variety, register, and genre according to audience, purpose, and setting.

Descriptor

- using the appropriate degree of formality with different audiences and settings

Progress Indicator

- participate in a group discussion using appropriate social behaviors (e.g., raising hand, taking turns, listening to others)

PROCEDURE

- Before starting this unit with students of varying abilities and grade levels, we make sure beginners know the names of the animals to be studied. Picture flash cards may be used for this purpose before the unit is started.

- We then show pictures of numerous types of eggs and ask students to tell us what they know about eggs. In our multiage, multiability-level class, the more advanced students tell what they know, and we then ask questions to encourage other students to participate. Some of the questions we use are

> What shape is this egg?
>
> Is this egg round or oval?
>
> What colors are the eggs?
>
> Are all the eggs the same?
>
> Are these eggs the same size?

Group Chart

<u>What Do You Know About Eggs?</u>
- Eggs are different sizes.
- Some eggs are white.
- Some are yellow or blue.
- All eggs are not the same.
- Yellow stuff (yolk*) is in the egg.
- White messy stuff (the egg white*) is there, too.
- Baby chicks come out of eggs.
- Chickens use their mouths (beaks*) to get out of (hatch from*) eggs.

What is inside of the egg?

What can we do with an egg?

How does the animal get out of the egg?

- Student responses, both self-generated and elicited, are listed on chart paper as we repeat the students' answers and create complete sentences. For example, "oval" may become "The egg is oval." The group chart on page 71 shows the results of the discussion.

One of the difficulties with students at this grade level is that they listen only when the teacher speaks. A goal of this lesson is to foster conversation and appropriate social interaction. The technique for eliciting from the students the items in the group chart will depend on the makeup of the class. We can supply the correct vocabulary after repeating a student's response. For example, "White, messy stuff" is repeated as "the egg white." Or the correct word can be elicited from the more proficient students in the group. Once one student generates the correct response, it is important to have other students repeat it. This can be done by asking, "Keiko, please tell me what Dmitriy said." In this way, students are encouraged to listen to each other.

- To continue eliciting background knowledge, we ask students to name the kinds of animals they know that come from eggs, such as ducks, chickens, snakes, and frogs. We list these responses on the "Animals That Come From Eggs" chart shown below. This also serves as an orientation to storybook reading, the next activity.

Animals That Come From Eggs

Animals That Come From Eggs

ducks	lizards
chickens	crocodiles
fish	alligators
turtles	frogs
birds	toads
snakes	seahorses
spiders	snails

- Using **shared reading** techniques, we next read to the class a general book about animals that come from eggs, using either a Grade 1 book, such as *Chickens Aren't the Only Ones* (Heller, 1981), or a Grade 2 book, such as *Hatched From an Egg* (Nelson, 1990), depending on the makeup of the class. Both books give students an overall view of different animals that come from eggs. After the book is read, students add to the list of animals that they started prior to reading the book. This provides a content-based extension activity and also closure to the book reading.

Beginning-level students are able to give the name of an animal to add to the list when we show a picture. More advanced students may not need to refer to the text. They may also be called upon to help beginners remember the name of a particular animal. For example, advanced-level students may say the name of a particular animal, and the beginning-level students may repeat the response.

Assessment

We informally review the vocabulary from this activity during the next lesson's warm-up or during a debriefing. For debriefing, animal names are reviewed as students leave the room. For example, students may be asked to answer questions appropriate to their proficiency levels about animals that come from eggs. Correct responses are their keys to open the gate to leave the room. Sometimes this activity can have a theme-related title. For example, for this unit, it could be called "Open the Barn Door."

Mac"Egg" Music: "Old MacDonald Had a Pond"

Songs are a good way to reinforce language. The song on page 75 is sung to the tune of "Old MacDonald Had a Farm," but has been rewritten to accompany this unit. It reinforces the names of animals and action words from the stories in the unit. We created the new song by substituting names of farm animals with the names of animals that come from eggs, and by retaining the rhythm of the original music.

Goal 1, Standard 3 **To use English to communicate in social settings: Students will use learning strategies to extend their communicative competence.**

Descriptors

- learning and using language "chunks"
- practicing new language

Progress Indicators

- recite poems or songs aloud or to oneself
- imitate a classmate's response to a teacher's directions

Goal 3, Standard 2 To use English in socially and culturally appropriate ways: Students will use nonverbal communication appropriate to audience, purpose, and setting.

Descriptors

- using acceptable tone, volume, stress, and intonation
- recognizing and adjusting behavior in response to nonverbal cues

Progress Indicators

- add gestures to correspond to words in a song
- use appropriate volume of voice in different settings

PROCEDURE

- We introduce and then practice the names of each animal and model the accompanying gestures for students. Beginning-level students can participate in this activity by following peers. Listed below are some of the animals and motions that we teach.

  duck: waddle, waddle

  turtle: snap, snap

  snake: slither, slither

  bird: flap, flap

  frog: hop, hop

  fish: swim, swim

  alligator: chomp, chomp

  bee: buzz, buzz

  butterfly: flutter, flutter

  chick: peck, peck

- We teach the song in small chunks throughout the unit and sing it often.

"Eggs"pressive Eggs: Introducing Descriptive Words and Language Patterns

The next book that we read is *Tap! Tap! The Egg Cracked* (Faulkner, 1992). In this book, a hen loses her first egg and rushes around to other nests looking for it. The hen remarks at each nest how the egg in the nest is different from her egg. The egg flips open, and the baby animal is revealed.

PROCEDURE

- We introduce new vocabulary within the context of the story. Intermediate-level students should learn the meaning of descriptive words such as *leathery, slippery,* or *wiggly.* These words can be demonstrated with hand and body gestures, or with realia such as a piece of leather. Beginning-level students may not yet know the names of all the animals, so

Old MacDonald Has a Pond

Old MacDonald has a pond, E-I-E-I-O
And in his pond he has a duck, E-I-E-I-O
With a "waddle-waddle" here and a "waddle-waddle" there
Here a "waddle" there a "waddle"
Everywhere a "waddle-waddle"
Old MacDonald has a pond, E-I-E-I-O
Old MacDonald has a pond, E-I-E-I-O
And in his pond he has a turtle, E-I-E-I-O
With a "snap-snap" here and a "snap-snap" there
Here a "snap" there a "snap"
Everywhere a "snap-snap"
With a "waddle-waddle" here and a "waddle-waddle" there
Here a "waddle" there a "waddle"
Everywhere a "waddle-waddle"
Old MacDonald has a pond, E-I-E-I-O
Old MacDonald has a pond, E-I-E-I-O
And in his pond he has a snake, E-I-E-I-O
With a "slither, slither" here and a "slither, slither" there
Here a "slither" there a "slither"
Everywhere a "slither, slither"
With a "snap-snap" here and a "snap-snap" there
Here a "snap" there a "snap"
Everywhere a "snap-snap"
With a "waddle-waddle" here and a "waddle-waddle" there
Here a "waddle" there a "waddle"
Everywhere a "waddle-waddle"
Old MacDonald has a pond, E-I-E-I-O

(Repeat using animals and actions from the list shown on p. 74)

Goal 2, Standard 2 **To use English to achieve academically in all content areas: Students will use English to obtain, process, construct, and provide subject matter information in spoken and written form.**

Descriptors

- formulating and asking questions
- hypothesizing and predicting
- selecting, connecting, and explaining information
- representing information visually

Progress Indicators

- make pictures to check comprehension of a story or process
- read a story and represent the sequence of events

we review this vocabulary. Students enjoy learning the repetitive phrases from the stories, such as "I wonder if that's my egg?" and "Tap! Tap! The egg cracked."

- After reading the books to students, we give them the blank egg patterns shown below. The students color the outside cutout the correct egg color. On the inside cutout they draw a picture of an animal in the egg. Various types of eggs from *Tap! Tap! The Egg Cracked* (Faulkner, 1992) are used. We explain to students that this is science and that they must use the colors shown in the book.

To adapt this activity for a group of second graders, we give each student a different egg pattern and instruct the students to color and draw the correct animal inside. Students in lower level groups may all complete the same egg patterns and put their eggs in an appropriate nest.

ASSESSMENT

There are a variety of assessments for different proficiency levels that can be used with this activity. High beginning-level students with more limited language can demonstrate knowledge of language and content through using repeated patterns in a guessing game. After the students finish their egg pictures, the eggs are put in the middle of the table. One student picks an egg and says, "I wonder if this is my egg?" The whole group responds "Tap! Tap! The egg cracked," and the student with the egg identifies what animal is in the egg. More advanced-level students can respond without the constraints of using a particular language pattern. They can describe what is different about the size, shape, and color of their particular eggs.

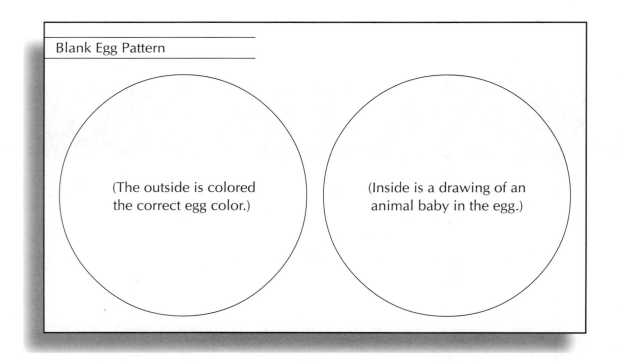

Blank Egg Pattern

(The outside is colored the correct egg color.)

(Inside is a drawing of an animal baby in the egg.)

Cre"Egg"tive Riddles: Writing and Answering Riddles

Creating riddles provides students with an opportunity to speak in front of the ESL group or their mainstream class. Because the language can be practiced ahead of time, students are generally eager to participate.

Although this activity requires creativity and thinking skills, the main purpose is to provide the students with practice presenting information to a group and being a good audience. We establish firm rules for appropriate responses to classmates' presentations and encourage active listening. Students rehearse giving compliments about the work of others.

Goal 1, Standard 3   To use English to communicate in social settings: Students will use learning strategies to extend their communicative competence.

Descriptor

- seeking support and feedback from others

Progress Indicator

- respond appropriately to classmates' work

Goal 3, Standard 1   To use English in socially and culturally appropriate ways: Students will use the appropriate language variety, register, and genre according to audience, purpose, and setting.

Descriptor

- using the appropriate degree of formality with different audiences and settings

Progress Indicator

- present a riddle in front of a group

Goal 3, Standard 2   To use English in socially and culturally appropriate ways: Students will use nonverbal communication appropriate to audience, purpose, and setting.

Descriptor

- using acceptable tone, volume, stress, and intonation in various social settings

Progress Indicator

- use appropriate volume of voice, stress, and intonation in the classroom

PROCEDURE

- On a double egg-shaped pattern that folds in half like a book, students write *This animal hatches from an egg. It can _____ and_____. What is it?* Students write their riddles on the outside egg pattern and draw pictures of their animals on the inside. For example, "This animal hatches from an egg. It can swim in the ocean and has sharp teeth." There is a picture of a shark inside. One student's egg riddle is shown below.

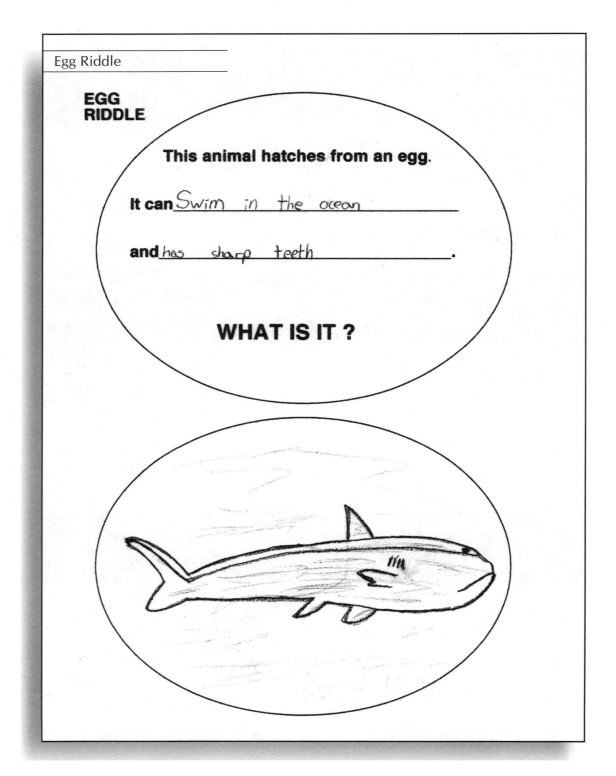

Egg Riddle

EGG RIDDLE

This animal hatches from an egg.

It can Swim in the ocean

and has sharp teeth.

WHAT IS IT ?

- Students read their riddles to the ESL group. They practice good oral delivery of their riddle. Their classmates are required to actively listen and ask questions if they are not able to guess the riddle. When the author is done, other students give compliments, using phrases such as "I like your shark. It is scary." These riddles can be displayed outside the ESL classroom for all students to enjoy.

ASSESSMENT

Assessment for this activity involves determining students' ability to understand socially and culturally appropriate behavior and evaluating students' understanding of content and their language use in developing a riddle. Evaluation of language includes use of correct information to complete the riddle accurately and the correct form of descriptive words to fit the compound sentence structure.

"Eggs"cellent Stories: Comparing Fact and Fiction

Our goal in this activity is to have students compare and contrast real and make-believe stories. It also focuses on the language students need for social interaction in the classroom to successfully complete their assignments.

Goal 1, Standard 3   To use English to communicate in social settings: Students will use learning strategies to extend their communicative competence.

Descriptors

- testing hypotheses about language
- learning and using language "chunks"

Progress Indicators

- repeat the sequence of a story
- test appropriate use of new phrases

Goal 2, Standard 1   To use English to achieve academically in all content areas: Students will use English to interact in the classroom.

Descriptors

- participating in full-class, group, and pair discussions
- negotiating and managing interaction to accomplish tasks

Progress Indicators

- join in group response at the appropriate time
- work with other students to complete a chart

Goal 2, Standard 2 To use English to achieve academically in all content areas: Students will use English to obtain, process, construct, and provide subject matter information in spoken and written form.

Descriptors

- interpreting information presented visually
- selecting, connecting, and explaining information

Progress Indicators

- construct a graphic showing data
- contrast and compare two stories
- explain change

PROCEDURE

- Before introducing the nonfiction book for this activity, we teach our students the concepts of *real* and *make-believe, fact* and *fiction.* This is an important concept taught at the end of first grade.

- To reinforce the concept of real and make-believe, we use pictures or sentence strips that show animals in real or make-believe situations. Some sentence strips are *The ducks swim in the pond. The chicken wears a red hat. The duck said, "I am going to eat."* Students work in pairs to sort the pictures or sentence strips under the headings "Real" and "Make-Believe." Student pairs take turns putting the strips or pictures in the appropriate column. The whole group is engaged in the lesson as they decide if the items are correctly placed.

- Next, the concept of real is reinforced by reading the fact book *Chicken and Egg* (Back & Olesen, 1986) to the class.

- One of the follow-up activities is to compare this book with *Tap! Tap! The Egg Cracked* (Faulkner, 1992). Students apply the concepts of real and make-believe as we compare the two books using a **Venn diagram**, such as the one shown on page 81 in "Comparing Real and Make-Believe."

- The book *Chicken and Egg* also lends itself to sequencing activities. Students

We make sure that we introduce whatever terms are being used by mainstream teachers. If the two grade levels use different terms, both sets are used.

We find that students of this age are helped by participating in the creation of a chart or graph, but they are usually unable to do so independently. Teacher questioning may be required to help students fill out the items in the Venn diagram. For example, "Is the chick doing something real or make-believe in this picture?"

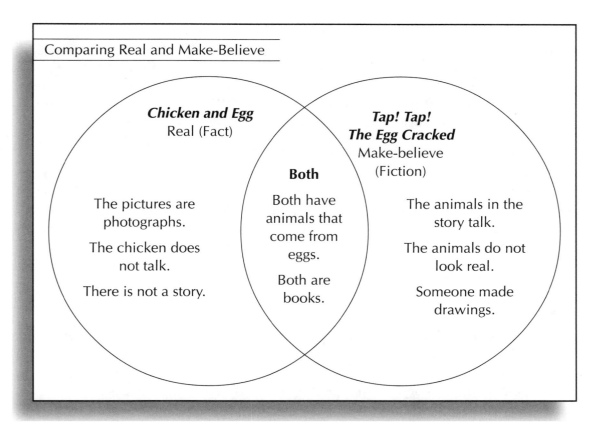

Comparing Real and Make-Believe

Chicken and Egg
Real (Fact)

The pictures are
photographs.

The chicken does
not talk.

There is not a story.

Both

Both have
animals that
come from
eggs.

Both are
books.

Tap! Tap!
The Egg Cracked
Make-believe
(Fiction)

The animals in the
story talk.

The animals do not
look real.

Someone made
drawings.

may draw the inside of an egg at different stages of the incubation period. They then describe the animal's growth inside the egg. For example, when the chicks are born, they cannot stand up, they do not have many feathers, and their eyes are closed. This is also a good time to talk about changes, asking students to compare the animal's growth with their own.

- Another type of sequencing we do with our students is a **movie frame graphic organizer**. Here, students put a set of pictures in order, using the book as reference. Students then practice the sequencing by orally telling what is happening in each picture. A sample sequence might be

> The hen lays the egg.
>
> You can see the chick's head and eye.
>
> The chick is almost ready to come out of the egg.
>
> The chick breaks the eggshell.
>
> The wet chick comes out of the eggshell.
>
> The chick is dry and fluffy.

Sequencing is a part of many content classroom activities. Students are expected to be able to sequence stories, steps in mathematical processes, and science observations. ESOL students preparing to participate in sequencing activities in the mainstream classroom need to practice them in the ESL classroom, first nonverbally and then verbally, as they become more proficient with language. We attempt to always meet students at their comfort levels of performance and work toward the next level.

ASSESSMENT

Recording observations of student performance in sequencing provides us with valuable assessment information about students' level of communicative behavior. If they are unable to sequence accurately, then communicative competence in ordinary classroom tasks is compromised. We see our students for only 30–45 minutes a day, so we share these observations and suggestions for practice with the students' mainstream teachers.

"Eggs"pressions: Connecting New Information to Information Previously Learned

Now we are ready to read some fiction books about ducks. *Have You Seen My Duckling?* (Tarfuri, 1986) is an easy K–1 book, and *Number Nine Duckling* (Akass, 1993) is a Grade 1 book. As we read books to our students, we continually ask them to hypothesize what they think the story will be about and what they think will happen next. With a more advanced-level group of students, we may read *Make Way for Ducklings* (McCloskey, 1941). This book is very challenging for ESOL students.

PROCEDURE

- We use *Have You Seen My Duckling?* as a wordless book to promote oral language. The more fluent students in the group supply a text for the pictures or add to the repeated line of text. Less fluent students are able to point to pictures and answer questions such as: "How many ducks are there? Are all of the ducks following the mother? Where is the last duckling? Is it following the mother?" Spatial concepts can be reviewed as students look for the missing duckling. This book can also be compared with *Tap! Tap! The Egg Cracked* (Faulkner, 1992).

Goal 1, Standard 1   **To use English to communicate in social settings: Students will use English to participate in social interactions.**

Descriptor
- expressing needs, feelings, and ideas

Progress Indicator
- describe feelings

Goal 2, Standard 2   **To use English to achieve academically in all content areas: Students will use English to obtain, process, construct, and provide subject matter information in spoken and written form.**

Descriptor
- hypothesizing and predicting

Progress Indicator
- explain change in a story

Goal 2, Standard 3 To use English to achieve academically in all content areas: Students will use appropriate learning strategies to construct and apply academic knowledge.

Descriptor

- actively connecting new information to information previously learned

Progress Indicator

- make pictures to check comprehension of a story or process

- *Number Nine Duckling* tells the story of a duck who is afraid to try anything new. All the ducks except for Number Nine Duckling jump down from the haystack where they were hatched. During the reading of the story, students make predictions about what happens next. Students also talk about the story parts and sequence the action. We like to make a display about this story for our bulletin board by drawing an egg carton with 12 places for eggs. Students write the name of the story, the author, the setting, the main characters, and six sentences retelling the story. They put one idea on each egg and place the eggs in order in the carton.

- We next ask students how they would feel if they were Number Nine Duckling. We brainstorm with students lists of things that made them afraid when they were younger but that they now know how to do. One list of "What Used to Make Me Afraid" is shown below.

What Used to Make Me Afraid

What Used to Make Me Afraid

riding a bike   playing soccer
roller skating   climbing trees
big kids   the dark

the first day of school
going outside at lunchtime
being left with the babysitter

- Another **graphic organizer** for Grades 1–2 can be constructed with adding-machine paper. Students who are advanced beginners and cannot write six sentences on their own can do the following in sequence on adding-machine paper: Copy the name of the story, the author's name, the setting, and the names of the main characters. Draw pictures of the story in sequence.

- Other activities for students with somewhat more advanced language skills can include drawing a picture of their favorite part of the book and giving one or more reasons it is a favorite.

ASSESSMENT

We assess students' understanding of this activity through a variety of extension activities. Beginning-level and less fluent students draw pictures of things that make them afraid and label them with a single word or phrase. More advanced-level students write about what used to make them afraid and why they are not afraid anymore. Another writing activity for all students is to ask them who might help Number Nine Duckling learn how to swim. For beginning-level students, we ask, "Can a sheep help the duckling learn how to swim?" Then students repeat in a chant, "No, a sheep can run and jump, but it can't swim." More advanced-level students brainstorm the types of animals that could teach Number Nine Duckling how to swim.

We also assess through observation how our students perform on these story extensions. These activities are also done within the Grade 1 and 2 classrooms, and thus need to be practiced and reinforced in ESL. We share with the classroom teacher our observations of student performance and suggestions of activities for further practice.

Science "Eggs"periments: Introducing the Scientific Method and Learning to Make Educated Guesses

Science experiments are a good way to reinforce sequencing, develop vocabulary, and introduce the scientific method to students. We also want to teach our students that it is permissible to make a wrong guess in science. This is a difficult concept for some of our Asian students, who have been schooled to always give the correct response. Students are not expected to master the terms of the scientific method.

> **Goal 2, Standard 2**   To use English to achieve academically in all content areas: Students will use English to obtain, process, construct, and provide subject matter information in spoken and written form.
>
> **Descriptors**
> - hypothesizing and predicting
> - formulating and asking questions
> - analyzing, synthesizing, and inferring from information
> - listening to and speaking about subject matter information
>
> **Progress Indicators**
> - record observations
> - use contextual clues

PROCEDURE, EXPERIMENT 1: "EGGS"AMINING EGGS: HOW TO TELL IF AN EGG IS COOKED

- Before this lesson is taught, students need to know the vocabulary *cooked* and *raw*. This is best demonstrated by showing them the inside of a hard-boiled and a raw egg. More advanced-level students can elaborate on the way the inside looks, smells, and feels in response to questions such as, "Do the cooked and raw eggs smell the same? How does the raw egg white feel? What color is the yolk? How does the cooked egg white feel?"

- We let students examine a cooked egg and a raw egg, which have been marked Egg A and Egg B. Can students tell the difference? Do the eggs feel different? Do they smell different? Do they look different? Do they sound different if shaken? We explain to students that this is what we want to find out during the experiment and that this is called the *question*. The question is written on the board: "Can we tell a cooked egg from a raw egg without breaking it?"

- Students then guess which egg is cooked, Egg A or Egg B, and their responses are written down. We explain that this is the *guess* or the *hypothesis* and that it does not have to be correct.

- We explain to students that the next part is the *procedure* or the steps of the experiment. This tells what you do first, second, third, and so forth.

    Spin the egg on its side very fast.

    Make it stop by pressing on it with your finger.

    Remove your finger quickly.

- The students observe that the raw egg will continue to spin. We explain that this is called the *result*, or what happened during the experiment.

- Students then tell why they think the raw egg continued to spin. We are satisfied with a simple explanation that the contents of the raw egg continue to move because it is not solid. A hard-boiled egg would not start again because its contents are solid. We explain to students that this is the *conclusion*, or what we learned during the experiment.

PROCEDURE, EXPERIMENT 2: "EGGS"TREMELY STRONG EGGS:
WHY DOESN'T A MOTHER HEN BREAK HER EGGS?

This experiment helps young children understand how a hen or a duck can sit on the eggs without breaking them. This is a common concern for children of this age. Students learn to discuss a scientific process and practice new language patterns. As we do the experiment, we **think aloud** to model the language.

- *Question*: Can six eggshells hold up three or four heavy dictionaries?

- *Hypothesis*: Students guess *yes* or *no*, and their guesses are recorded.

- *Materials*: six large eggs, scissors, a cup, three or four dictionaries, masking tape We tell students that the materials are things needed to do the experiment.

- *Procedure*:

    1. Crack each egg and empty the yolk in a cup.

    2. Wash the eggshells and let them dry.

3. Cut the edges of the eggshells with scissors and cover them with masking tape.

4. Arrange the eggshells in a square and put one dictionary on top.

At this point, we ask students if they would like to change their guess, while showing them that there are still two to three dictionaries to put on top of the eggshells. Most students will want to change their guess. We explain that this is what an experiment is: to make a guess about something, to try out something new, and to change the guess if you need to.

- *Results*: The eggshells do not break.
- *Conclusion*: The arc-like shape of the egg helps support the weight of the dictionaries. The shape of the egg is the reason the mother duck or hen does not break it when she sits on it.

ASSESSMENT

To assess students' understanding of the experiment, we ask them to sequence the steps in the experiment using pictures or short sentences, depending on their grade and ability level.

PROCEDURE, EXPERIMENT 3: "EGGS"CEPTIONAL BOUNCING EGGS: CAN YOU MAKE AN EGG BOUNCE?

- *Question*: Can you make an egg bounce?
- *Hypothesis*: Students make guesses and their hypotheses are written down.
- *Materials*: hard-boiled eggs, white vinegar, jar or large cup, and water
- *Procedure*:
    1. Soak eggs for 48–72 hours in white vinegar until all of the shell is removed.
    2. Soak in water overnight.
    3. Have students lightly drop the egg on a table from 2 or 3 feet above.
- *Result*: The egg does not break. It bounces.
- *Conclusion*: The vinegar removes the shell but leaves the membrane or skin. The water stretches the membrane. (The membrane is thick and can be shown to students.) This allows the egg to bounce.

ASSESSMENT

We ask students to draw and label the steps of the experiment. We also have them compare a peeled, hard-boiled egg with their bouncing egg. Do the eggs look and feel different? Do they smell different? Where is the membrane on the hard-boiled egg? This question helps students understand why the membrane on the bouncing egg is strong.

Another way to assess students' understanding of these experiments is to give each student a large 6-in.-by-9-in. index card or a 9-in.-by-12-in. sheet of construction paper with one step of an experiment written on it. Students must draw pictures of their steps. Finally, the group decides which sentence best describes the conclusion. They label this picture with the word Conclusion. Students then place the pictures in the correct order. This can be done on a large table.

Students present their bouncing egg experiment to their mainstream classes. They pose the question "Do you think this egg will bounce?" and then demonstrate the experiment. After they have completed an oral presentation, the index cards will be glued to their poster boards, and the poster boards can be hung in the hallway for other students in the school to see.

"Eggs"act Math Activity: Favorite Egg Survey

Surveys are a way to encourage students to interact with their mainstream classmates. They give students a chance to use language chunks, which they have practiced in advance. Although this activity has a content component, students' attention is mostly focused on oral language development and social interaction.

Goal 1, Standard 2   To use English to communicate in social settings: Students will interact in, through, and with spoken and written English for personal expression and enjoyment.

Descriptors
- describing and participating in a favorite activity
- sharing cultural traditions
- expressing feelings and ideas
- participating in popular culture

Progress Indicators
- respond to a survey
- ask information questions for personal reasons
- talk about a favorite food

Goal 2, Standard 2   To use English to achieve academically in all content areas: Students will use English to obtain, process, construct, and provide subject matter information in spoken and written form.

Descriptor
- representing information visually and interpreting information presented visually

Progress Indicators
- construct a chart synthesizing information
- compare responses
- record information accurately

PROCEDURE

- In this part of the unit, students brainstorm different ways that eggs are eaten. If they do not have much experience cooking and eating eggs, we bring in samples of eggs cooked in different ways for them to try. We want to have four different ways to cook eggs.

"Eggs"act Math Survey										
Hard-boiled										
Scrambled										
Fried										
Soft-boiled										
Raw										
Other										
	1	2	3	4	5	6	7	8	9	10

- We make a chart with 11 horizontal boxes and 7 vertical boxes, as shown on the "'Eggs'act Math" chart above. Students fill in the boxes in the first column with the names of the four types of eggs they brainstormed and draw small pictures of them beside the names. For example, for a hard-boiled egg, they might draw a decorated Easter egg; for a soft-boiled egg, they could draw an egg in an eggcup; fried eggs can be shown with a sunny-side-up egg; and scrambled eggs can be shown in a frying pan.

- We then give students clipboards and pencils and have them practice asking other members of the ESL class, "What is your favorite kind of egg?" The students interviewed write their names in the same row as their favorite eggs. We show students that only one name goes in each box on their charts. We then take students on a trip around the school so they can practice asking other people this question. This serves as a model when they return to their classrooms to survey their classmates.

- The next day the students bring in their completed surveys and combine their findings into a group graph. This is a good time to review expressions such as *more than, less than, the most,* and *the least.* If these concepts have not been previously taught, they can be taught from the graphs.

ASSESSMENT

We assess students through their oral responses to questions about the graph, such as "Which type of egg did most people like? Which type of egg did the fewest people like?" We expect more advanced-level students to write or say their own sentences about the graph, using expressions such as *more than, less than, the most,* and *the least.*

"Eggs"emplary Writing: Building Self-Esteem Through Reflective Writing: I Am a Good Egg

Most young ESOL students need help in building a positive self-image. This next activity is important because many children from other cultures are not used to talking about their good qualities. They often do not feel that they are worthy subjects of a writing piece or that their individual feelings count.

> **Goal 1, Standard 1** To use English to communicate in social settings: Students will use English to participate in social interactions.
>
> **Descriptor**
> - sharing and requesting information
>
> **Progress Indicator**
> - respond to questions about self

> **Goal 3, Standard 1** To use English in socially and culturally appropriate ways: Students will use the appropriate language variety, register, and genre according to audience, purpose, and setting.
>
> **Descriptors**
> - responding to and using idioms appropriately
> - using a variety of writing styles appropriate for different audiences, purposes, and settings
>
> **Progress Indicators**
> - demonstrate an understanding of the way to express feelings
> - use idioms appropriately

Procedure

- We explain to students that a *good egg* is someone who is kind and nice to have as a friend, and model examples by using ourselves or one of the students: "Akiko is a good egg because she helped Min Hee with her math." Students brainstorm why they are good eggs by saying what they have done recently to help someone. Some of their ideas are shown on the "I Am a Good Egg Because I . . ." chart on page 90.

This is another good exercise for a multilevel group. Some students will only be able to draw pictures and copy a sentence. Others will be able to write a short paragraph and illustrate.

I Am a Good Egg Because I . . .

I am a good egg because I ..

- helped someone learn English
- played with someone who was alone

- helped my friend with math
- shared my toys with friends
- made a friend feel better when she was crying

- Students generate many thoughts once they get the idea. We give everyone a sheet of writing paper that we have cut in an egg shape and have them write why they are

Technology has added a great deal to what we can do with student pictures. At the beginning of the school year, we take a picture of each student. These pictures are scanned into a file on the computer and kept for use during the year. Individual class pictures can also be scanned. When we want colored pictures of students for a project, we can print out the photographs to use.

More advanced-level students who can write enjoy a collective type of good-egg activity. Students cut out large egg-shaped patterns and put their pictures in the center. Students write on their own eggs, "_____ is a good egg because . . . ." and pass the eggs to the person on their right. Each student has a different colored marker. Eggs are passed around, and students write about their classmates as they complete the statements. They practice saying positive things about each other and may not repeat an item that has already been used. At the end of the session, students have their own eggs, with positive statements from their classmates written on them.

good eggs using the sentence starter: "[Student name and picture] is a good egg because . . . ." When the students write their final version, we back each sheet with egg-shaped colored construction paper.

"Eggs"cursion Scavenger Hunt: Unit Assessment

This activity helps the teacher assess student knowledge and can be used as a culminating activity for the unit.

Goal 2, Standard 1 To use English to achieve academically in all content areas: Students will use English to interact in the classroom.

Descriptors

- negotiating and managing interaction to accomplish tasks
- elaborating and extending other people's ideas and words
- participating in full-class, group, and pair discussions

Progress Indicators

- share classroom materials and work successfully with a partner
- collect and return classroom materials
- join in a group response at the appropriate time

Goal 2, Standard 3 To use English to achieve academically in all content areas: Students will use appropriate learning strategies to construct and apply academic knowledge.

Descriptors

- focusing attention selectively
- applying self-monitoring and self-correcting strategies to build and expand a knowledge base

Progress Indicators

- take risks with language
- rephrase, explain, revise, and expand oral or written information to check comprehension
- seek more knowledgeable others with whom to consult to advance understanding

PROCEDURE

- Using colored plastic Easter eggs, we put a slip of paper in each egg with a question from the unit written on it. The eggs are then hidden in the classroom, on the playground, or throughout a section of the school building.
- We divide students into pairs, trying to match a nonreader with a reader so they can work together. We also tell each pair how many eggs they should find.

- Then the students hunt for the eggs and bring them back to their seats.
- Each pair reads their questions aloud and gives answers. If they do not know the correct answer, the other pairs have a chance to steal the point.
- Although we keep score on the chalkboard, we make sure everyone is a winner by giving all students egg stickers or small egg-shaped erasers as rewards.

ASSESSMENT

This activity assesses numerous areas:

1. knowledge of the unit content (What do students understand and remember?)
2. ability to paraphrase learned information (Can students repeat information in their own words?)
3. growth in language (How do students take risks in an informal lesson?)
4. culturally appropriate response (Have students learned to take turns, use correct register and volume, and listen when others speak?)
5. appropriate use of classroom materials (Have students learned the correct behavior involved in finding, gathering, and returning classroom materials?)

Conclusions

As a way of drawing our unit to a close, we include a plan for a week's worth of lessons. Because of the time constraints of the 30- to 45-minute pullout sessions, it is often difficult in low-incidence settings to predict how many of a unit's activities can be accomplished in 1 week. Additionally, when introducing new concepts to students in this age range, we are sometimes surprised to discover how much more time it takes to help students understand, learn, and remember new concepts and new language. Because we only see our students once a day, daily reviews help students activate their prior knowledge and newly learned information from one day to the next. On the lesson plan shown on page 93, we have charted a cluster of activities from this unit that may be accomplished in 1 week's time.

RESOURCES AND REFERENCES

Children's Literature

Fiction

Akass, S. (1993). *Number nine duckling.* Honesdale, PA: Boyd's Mill Press.
 A duckling learns he can do anything if he sets his mind to it.

Faulkner, K. (1992). *Tap! tap! The egg cracked.* Hampshire, England: Brainwaves.
 A mother hen loses her egg and searches for it in the nests of other animals.

Heller, R. (1981). *Chickens aren't the only ones.* New York: Scholastic.
 This is a lively introduction to animals that hatch from eggs.

McCloskey, R. (1941). *Make way for ducklings.* New York: Viking Press.
 This is the classic story of the mother duck who guides her ducklings through the streets of Boston, with some help from a Boston policeman.

Tarfuri, N. (1986). *Have you seen my duckling?* New York: Greenwillow Books.
 A mother duck leads her brood around a pond as she searches for a missing duckling.

Lesson Plan	
Monday **Grades 1–2**	Lesson objectives: Introduce Animal "Eggs"amination • elicit students' prior knowledge of eggs • write information on chart in sentence form • discuss and repeat information about eggs • debrief using "Magic Gate"
Tuesday **Grades 1–2**	Lesson objectives: Introduce storybook to give students background on animals that come from eggs; introduce song to students • read story to students • list and discuss animals that come from eggs • review list and link to information elicited previously • introduce the words of first verse of "Old MacDonald"
Wednesday **Grades 1–2**	Lesson objectives: Introduce cross-content story *Tap! Tap!*; describe different eggs • read story to students • discuss and illustrate terms: *slippery*, *wiggly*, and *leathery* • reread story having individual students say repetitive phrases • summary/assessment: demonstrate new vocabulary and have students guess the word • repeat part of a phrase and have students complete it ("I wonder if . . . " or "Tap! Tap! . . . ")
Thursday **Grades 1–2**	Lesson objectives: Review animals and their eggs; draw eggshells and baby animals inside • review/assessment: discuss color, shape, size, and texture of each animal's egg • show egg patterns and explain project; review steps • explain how each student is now a scientist; have students create their own eggs using authentic colors/drawings
Friday **Grades 1–2**	Lesson objectives: Review week's lessons; add to and practice song • assessment: students review week's activities • students guess what kind of animal is in classmates' eggs • artist/expert explains his/her egg to group • add verses to "Old MacDonald" and practice with students

Nonfiction

Back, C., & Olesen, J. (1986). *Chicken and egg*. Morristown, NJ: Silver Burdett Press. *Photographs, drawings, and text follow the development of a chick embryo from the fertilization and laying of an egg to the time a chick hatches.*

Biddulph, F., & Biddulph, J. (1992). *Spiders are special animals*. Bothell, WA: The Wright Group. *This book is an overview of the physical characteristics and activities of spiders.*

Clark, P. (1995). *Insects and spiders.* New York: Franklin Watts.
  Photographs and text describe the physical characteristics, lifestyles, and environmental effects of ants, beetles, flies, and spiders.

Holloway, J., & Harper, C. (1993). *Amphibians are animals.* Cleveland, OH: Modern Curriculum Press.
  Children are introduced to the general characteristics of amphibians.

Holloway, J., & Harper, C. (1993). *Birds are animals.* Cleveland, OH: Modern Curriculum Press.
  Children are introduced to the general characteristics of birds.

Holloway, J., & Harper, C. (1993). *Insects are animals.* Cleveland, OH: Modern Curriculum Press.
  Children are introduced to the general characteristics of insects.

Julivert, M. (1991). *The fascinating world of ants.* Hauppauge, NY: Barron's Educational Series.
  This book describes the appearance, life cycle, activities, and social habits of ants.

Julivert, M. (1991). *The fascinating world of snakes.* Hauppauge, NY: Barron's Educational Series.
  This book describes the physical characteristics, behavior, and habitats of various kinds of snakes.

Nelson, J. (1990). *Hatched from an egg.* Cleveland, OH: Modern Curriculum Press.
  This science story introduces the various animals that lay eggs.

Selsam, M. (1970). *Egg to chick.* New York: Harper & Row.
  This book traces the development of a chick from fertilization until the baby chick pecks its way through the shell.

Sheridan, J. (1992). *Ants, ants, ants.* Bothell, WA: The Wright Group.
  This is an overview of the physical characteristics of ants.

Sheridan, J. (1992). *How ants live.* Bothell, WA: The Wright Group.
  This is a description of ants' habitats and how they lay and care for eggs.

Stone, L. M. (1990). *Chickens.* Vero Beach, FL: Rourke.
  This book contains an introduction to the physical characteristics, habits, and natural environments of chickens.

Stone, L. M. (1990). *Ducks.* Vero Beach, FL: Rourke.
  This book contains an introduction to the physical characteristics, habits, and natural environments of ducks.

Watts, S. (1989). *Honeybee.* Englewood Cliffs, NJ: Silver Burdett Press.
  This book describes the life cycle and behavior of the honeybee.

Teacher Resources

Animals. (1994). Palos Verdes, CA: Frank Schaffer.
  This activity book contains theme ideas for young children studying animals.

Bingham, J., & Rawson, C. (1996). *The Usborne book of science experiments.* London: Usborne.
  This resource book provides information about science experiments for teachers and students.

Chamot, A. U., & O'Malley, J. M. (1994). *The CALLA handbook: Implementing the cognitive academic language learning approach.* Reading, MA: Addison-Wesley.
  This resource is a comprehensive handbook, based on O'Malley and Chamot's learning strategies research, for teaching second languages through core curriculum content instruction.

Eggs. (1990). Cypress, CA: Creative Teaching Press.
  This activity book contains theme ideas for young children to study eggs.

Koch, M. (1992). *Bird, egg, feather, nest.* New York: Stewart, Tabori & Chang.
  Remarkable facts about birds from all over the world are portrayed in watercolor images and with handwritten text.

O'Malley, J. M., & Pierce, L. V. (1996). *Authentic assessment for English language learners.* Reading, MA: Addison-Wesley.
  This is a companion resource to The CALLA Handbook, *exploring various tools for and approaches to content language assessment for oral language, reading, and writing.*

Ontario Science Centre. (1986). *Scienceworks*. Reading, MA: Addison-Wesley.
   This book of science experiments for elementary-age students is a resource for preparing science experiments in the classroom.

TESOL. (1997). *ESL standards for pre-K–12 students*. Alexandria. VA: Author.

Wellnitz, W. (1990). *Science magic for kids: 68 simple and safe experiments*. New York: TAB Books.
   Easy science experiments for young children are described in this book.

UNIT 5
Exploring Native American Cultures: The Iroquois

CARRIE MARTIN

Introduction

Walking into the classroom, you see all 30 second-grade students gathered into Iroquois families of four around the room. Some groups are on the floor, some are at desks grouped together, while others are at extra tables. Each group has a family folder containing sheets of paper with descriptions of each family member's role. The student leaders have already assigned and passed out family role pages to each group member.

You hear the families actively discussing and deciphering the particular roles of each Iroquois family member. The teacher walks from group to group, answering any questions the students may have. You see and hear students speaking and listening to each other as well as depending on one another for information about each of the family members. Students are learning language through cultural content.

Unit Overview

There are two main reasons why I chose to do a unit on the Iroquois. First, textbooks used for social studies instruction do not provide ample support for ESOL students, especially those at beginning levels of language proficiency. And second, the many Native American units written about various tribes do not address the needs of ESOL

Context

Grade level: Second grade

English proficiency levels: Mixed, beginner to fluent

Native languages of students: Approximately 90% Spanish, 10% English

Focus of instruction: Teaching English through social studies content

Type of class: Self-contained, grade-level class

Length of unit: 3–4 weeks

learners. The study of a northeastern woodland tribe will help my students relate to Native American cultures living in an environment that the students may not have experienced.

For purposes of time and space, I have focused my unit on the broader perspective of this culture. I divided the theme into three parts: the Iroquois home as Lesson 1, the Iroquois way of life as Lesson 2, and integrating the Iroquois culture with others as Lesson 3. Students get a global sense of the Iroquois culture in Lessons 1 and 2, and apply knowledge from these lessons in Lesson 3, where I introduce the six Iroquois nations (Cayuga, Mohawk, Oneida, Onondaga, Tuscarora, and Seneca). With each lesson having its own theme, I wrote the activities in the order they needed to be presented for that lesson. Each lesson should also be taught in sequential order.

Most students in my classroom, as well as in my school, are Spanish speaking. Due to the rapidly growing numbers of limited- and non-English speakers in our district and state, all teachers are required to have additional training in working with ESOL students, known as the cross-cultural language acquisition development (CLAD) credential. Thus, all teachers are considered to be ESL teachers and are expected to integrate language development strategies into their everyday teaching. The unit is therefore designed for a mainstream classroom with a majority of ESOL or English language development (ELD) children, but is also adaptable for a pullout ESL classroom or a second-grade classroom with a majority of native speakers of English (NSs).

This unit can be done any time throughout the school year. A teacher and class spending approximately 50–60 minutes daily and working in sequence as the activities are presented will complete the unit within 3–4 weeks. The amount of time spent will depend on the students' interest in the topic, the teacher's decisions about how much time to allow to complete activities, the time needed for review, and the length of the class periods.

The unit overview on page 99 shows a thematic web of the unit activities.

Standards

Whenever I start to plan a unit, I begin by creating a mind map of all the topics I want to teach. After gathering my materials and resources, I start to piece together the activities and examine which activities are necessary for my unit. In order to have a sense of purpose about a unit, however, it is important to have standards to give the supporting activities a solid foundation. Before I can plan the activities, I realize I need to make sure my activities are compatible with standards.

In writing this unit, I considered several sets of standards. Because the main purpose of this unit is to improve English for nonnative speakers (NNSs), *ESL Standards for Pre-K–12 Students* (TESOL, 1997) is the primary resource. I needed to become familiar enough with the ESL standards to be able to choose teaching strategies and activities that would best meet those standards as well as accommodate my theme and the needs of my students. I then created assessment tools based on the activities. Although integrating the ESL standards in this way was time consuming, I am confident it gave my unit the solidity and strength it needed.

To complement the ESL standards, I created an assessment tool that measures a student's ability to successfully meet a particular standard. The progress indicator chart, which is shown on page 100, has the standards organized by lessons, with the corresponding progress indicators listed below each standard. The number of the activity in which the standard is met is also given. I organized the chart in this fashion because I needed a way of seeing exactly when and where the assessment would best fit within

Unit Overview: Exploring Native American Cultures

*Final project

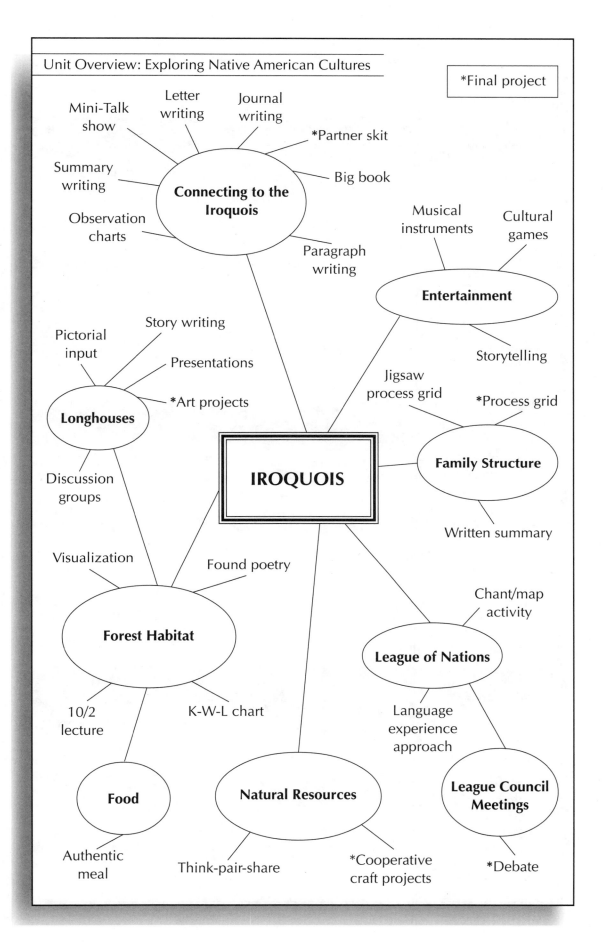

Mini-Talk show
Letter writing
Journal writing
*Partner skit
Summary writing
Big book
Observation charts

Connecting to the Iroquois

Paragraph writing

Musical instruments
Cultural games

Entertainment

Storytelling

Pictorial input
Story writing
Presentations
*Art projects

Longhouses

Discussion groups

Jigsaw process grid
*Process grid

IROQUOIS

Family Structure

Written summary

Visualization
Found poetry

Forest Habitat

Chant/map activity

League of Nations

10/2 lecture
K-W-L chart

Language experience approach

Food

Natural Resources

League Council Meetings

Authentic meal

Think-pair-share

*Cooperative craft projects

*Debate

Progress Indicator Chart

Student Name: _____

Lesson 1 Goal/Standard	Activity	Observation		
G1, S1		**Always**	**Sometimes**	**Rarely**
Engage listener's attention	1.2			
Ask clarification questions	1.1			
	1.4			
Offer/respond to compliments	1.1			
G2, S2				
Sequence events	1.8			
Gather information	1.3			
Use contextual clues	1.5			
G3, S3				
Observe language use	1.1			
	1.6			

Lesson 2 Goal/Standard	Activity	Observation		
G1, S2		**Always**	**Sometimes**	**Rarely**
Listen/respond to stories	2.1			
Enjoy games	2.5			
Talk about favorite food	2.8			
G2, S3				
Rehearse information	2.3			
Take risks	2.2			
Seek knowledge from others	2.4			
G3, S2				
Respond to teacher	any			
Get teacher's attention	any			

Lesson 3 Goal/Standard	Activity	Observation		
G1, S3		**Always**	**Sometimes**	**Rarely**
Test new language	3.5			
Connect pictures to labels	3.1			
G2, S1				
Join group discussion	3.4			
Work with partner	3.8			
G3, S1				
Write letter to adult	3.7			
Greet and leave	any			

the unit. I also used this chart to show growth in the standards from this unit to another unit with the same criteria.

During each activity, I carefully observed each student's ability to meet each standard. I kept a three-ring binder that contained copies of the progress indicator chart for each student in my class. During class time, I made anecdotal notes on a separate piece of paper. I also used students' work to find evidence of meeting the standards. Later, I transferred the information to each student's chart. Making notes during class time, as well as using students' completed work, helped me be more objective in my assessments.

To include the state and district standards, I tailored my theme at the start to ensure that I was teaching content for the appropriate grade level. Because my students spanned all proficiency levels, it was important for me to choose activities that were flexible enough to meet my ESOL students' needs as well as the needs of the NSs, the gifted students, and those with learning disabilities. I relied on the California State *History/Social Science Content Standards Grades K–12* (State of California, State Board of Education, 1998) to develop activities to help students

- understand basic economic concepts and their individual roles in the economy, and demonstrate basic economic reasoning skills in terms of how limits on resources require people to choose what to produce and what to consume

- demonstrate map skills by describing the absolute and relative locations of people, places, and environments by labeling a simple map from memory of the North American continent, including the countries, oceans, Great Lakes, major rivers, and mountain ranges; and by identifying the essential map elements of title, legend, directional indicator, scale, and map

I also used the district standards (Ontario/Montclair School District, 1999) to adapt activities for more advanced-level ESOL students and NSs. The goals of the district standards, which incorporate goals similar to those of the state standards, are for students to

- begin to appreciate the importance of individuals from many cultures, now and long ago

- participate in varied activities throughout the curriculum that promote respect and understanding for human commonalities and differences

Using a combination of the ESL standards, state standards, and district standards, I created a unit that would benefit students at all fluency levels as well as NSs in my classroom setting.

Lesson 1 Activities: The Iroquois Home

KEY VOCABULARY

forest	Iroquois
habitat	longhouse

MATERIALS

observation charts
forest mural
CD player
nature CD
chart paper

Goal 1, Standard 1 To use English to communicate in social settings: Students will use English to participate in social interactions.

Descriptors

- sharing and requesting information
- engaging in conversations

Progress Indicators

- engage listener's attention verbally or nonverbally
- elicit information and ask clarification questions
- offer and respond to compliments

Goal 2, Standard 2 To use English to achieve academically in all content areas: Students will use English to obtain, process, construct, and provide subject matter information in spoken and written form.

Descriptors

- gathering information orally and in writing
- retelling information
- responding to the work of peers and others
- understanding and producing technical vocabulary and text features according to content area

Progress Indicators

- sequence events of a story through pictures or words
- gather and organize the appropriate materials needed to complete a task
- use contextual clues

Goal 3, Standard 3 To use English in socially and culturally appropriate ways: Students will use appropriate learning strategies to extend their sociolinguistic and sociocultural competence.

Descriptors

- observing and modeling how others speak and behave in a particular situation or setting
- experimenting with variations of language in social and academic settings

Progress Indicator

- observe language use and behaviors of peers in different settings

Activity 1.1: Observation Charts

This activity served as a means to arouse students' curiosity about the Native American culture they were about to study.

PROCEDURE

- I placed several collage posters around the classroom, each with a particular theme about the Iroquois Indians. One poster contained pictures of longhouses, another contained examples of things in the forest habitat, another had illustrations of the Iroquois playing different games. There were also posters of clothing and family members interacting.

- I divided the class into heterogeneous groups for each poster.

- I gave students blank sheets of 8.5-in. x 11-in. paper and instructed them to fold their papers into fourths. I gave them approximately 1 minute to study their posters and another minute or so to write down in one quarter of their papers some words, phrases, or sentences expressing what the poster was about.

- When finished, each group moved to a different poster, rotating until they had seen each one.

- We then revisited each poster, allowing volunteers to voice what they noticed about the Iroquois in the pictures.

- I collected students' papers to pass back and add to in Lesson 3.

Activity 1.2: Visualization Using Realia and Pictorials

When teaching a culture, I always start with a motivational strategy that gives students an opportunity to imagine the habitat where that culture lives. This activity is particularly important for students who have not experienced a particular environment.

PROCEDURE

- I asked the students to close their eyes while I rolled out a mural that I had drawn on a large piece of paper (shown on p. 104). On the mural were rolling hills, trees, winding rivers, and clear lakes of the northeast. I placed the mural on the northeast side of the classroom to reinforce direction.

- I played a nature CD (Griswold, 1994) with the sounds of running water and birds singing and asked the students to pretend they were in a faraway place.

- When they opened their eyes, I asked them to guess where they were by discussing the sights and sounds with a neighbor.

- I concluded with a group discussion about the experience, telling them that on the northeast coast of the country, there are forests like this one where the Iroquois Indians used to live.

Activity 1.3: K-W-L Chart

I used the **K-W-L chart** to see how much the students as a group retained from the first two activities; the chart also helped me determine what prior knowledge students had, in addition to my introduction, and see what they still needed to learn about the forest. This information was helpful in figuring how much time we needed to spend on the forest habitat in the next activity.

Northeast Landscape Mural

PROCEDURE

- I placed on the board a large sheet of white poster paper already divided into three columns (K, W, L) representing the questions "What Do We *K*now?," "What Do We *W*ant to Learn?," and "What Did We *L*earn?."

- I asked students to tell me what they knew about the forest and wrote their responses in the *K* column.

- Then I asked them to tell me what they wanted to know about the forest and wrote their questions in the *W* column.

- Finally, we orally reviewed the two completed columns. I told students that during the next few weeks we would be studying a lot about the forest and the living things there.

- We revisited the K-W-L chart in Lesson 3 to fill in the *L* column.

Activity 1.4: 10/2 Lecture

This **10/2 lecture** activity was beneficial for students at all proficiency levels because it enabled them to learn the content needed to be successful with the activities that followed.

PROCEDURE

- Asking students to listen to find out what things live in the forest, I read a story about the forest to the class, entitled *Nature's Great Balancing Act* (Norsgaard, 1990).

- Every 10 minutes, I stopped reading to allow the students to talk with a neighbor for 2 minutes about what they just heard in the story.

- After I finished the story, I asked the students to identify things found in a forest. As they identified the living things, specifically ones useful to the Iroquois Indians, I held up corresponding word cards that I had prepared and asked students to repeat the words.

- Once the students had identified all the words, I displayed the cards on a word wall.

Activity 1.5: Found Poetry

This activity gave students an opportunity to learn high-level vocabulary on the subject and to internalize the new words and create new literature with them.

PROCEDURE

- First, I chose an excerpt from a documentary about forests from the National Geographic Society's Web site (Cochran, 1997). This Web site includes photos of the dense forests in West Virginia with natural recordings of the forest, including singing birds and rustling trees. By clicking on boxes embedded in the photos, I could view close-up shots of things in the forest and read short excerpts written about the close-ups. I chose a photo of the canopy of an 86-year-old forest. It described in four sentences the many layers of the forest as well as the variety of living things that inhabit each layer.

- Next, I created an overhead transparency based on the documentary excerpt on the forest. We read the transparency together as a class, and I asked the students to identify words that were scientific, interesting, or new to them, words that they would want to find out more about.

Found Poetry

Word List:

maturing	understory	sheltering
complex	canopy	eldest
multistoried	nests	wood thrush
habitats	tier	elsewhere
		among

Poem:

The Forest
Complex, Multistoried
Sheltering, Maturing, Sharing
A wood thrush makes nests.
Habitat

- As the students identified words, I underlined them on the transparency. We then copied the words onto cards and placed the cards in a pocket chart.

- Next, I placed students in pairs and gave each pair a card to research. The students used the classroom computer, dictionaries, encyclopedias, and me as a resource for learning their new words. Each pair then presented their word and its meaning to the class.

- The class then decided to sort the words into categories of nouns, adjectives, and verbs. They felt this would help them decide what kind of poem to write. After they decided to write a cinquain, or five-line stanza, they worked in groups of four to choose words from the transparency that would best represent the forest.

- With these words, we created a class poem about the forest. When we completed the poem, I typed and copied it, and distributed the copies to the students for reading practice. The "Found Poetry" they created as a class is shown on page 105.

Activity 1.6: Discussion Groups

This activity helped students use critical thinking to solve problems within the context of the unit.

PROCEDURE

- I gathered the students around the mural from the first activity and asked them to guess what materials they would use to make a house if they lived in this forest environment.

- I divided the class into heterogeneous groups of four and gave them approximately 10 minutes to brainstorm some ideas on paper.

- We met again as a whole class, and each group shared its ideas. I wrote three answers from each group on the board. We then decided as a class which answer was most likely the correct one for the Iroquois Indians.

- We concluded that the best answer was wood from trees. If the class had by chance not come up with the correct answer, I would have used this as an opportunity to revisit the facts on the forest.

Activity 1.7: Pictorial Input

I used this teaching strategy to demonstrate to students how the Iroquois Indians created a home for themselves using trees and other things from the forest. This strategy worked particularly well because the visual impact of the pictures I drew helped my students more easily remember the content.

PROCEDURE

- I divided my class into homogeneous groups with respect to students' English proficiency levels. This allowed me to be more descriptive with the beginning-level groups and less descriptive with the more advanced-level groups.

- Before the activity, I drew a picture of a longhouse for each group. Around the longhouse, I wrote notes that I wanted to share with each group of students. Both the drawing and the notes were in pencil so students could not see them from where they were sitting.

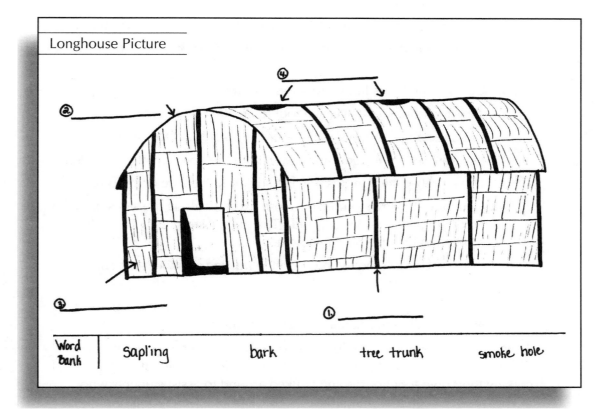

Longhouse Picture

Word Bank | Sapling   bark   tree trunk   smoke hole

- I then presented the drawing to each group, tracing over each part of it with a marker as I discussed the notes I had written. This procedure made the drawing look as if it magically appeared before the students' eyes.

- After I finished, the students reviewed what I had told them. I gave them copies of my longhouse picture (shown above) and asked them to label the parts we had talked about.

Activity 1.8: Art Projects

I used this activity as an opportunity for students to actually make a longhouse and see it in three dimensions. This activity gave my students a feel for what it must have been like for the Iroquois to make their houses.

PROCEDURE

- Before starting, I showed students the picture of the longhouse I had drawn from the previous activity and various pictures of longhouses found in books.

- I passed back students' papers from the previous activity and asked them to recite the steps needed to make a longhouse. I wrote them on the board and then demonstrated the procedure using the following supplies and steps.

> Supplies:
> stick pretzels (about 50 per student)
> thin black licorice (2 per student)
> scotch tape
> chocolate frosting
> small cereal boxes

1. Cut the front off the cereal box; save this piece to arch over the roof.

2. Lay the box down on its open side with the back facing up as the roof.

3. Cut two fire holes in the front piece of the cereal box from Step 1.

4. Tape the front piece over the roof to create a slight arch.

5. Cut a rectangle in the short side of the box for a door.

6. Lay the box on its open side again, with the door facing the student.

7. Dip a pretzel stick in frosting and stick it to the side of the box.

8. Continue sticking the pretzels close together along the sides of the box until the sides are covered. (The pretzel sticks may be broken or nibbled to the appropriate length.)

9. Cover the entire roof with chocolate frosting (making sure not to cover the fire holes).

10. Lay black licorice pieces across the width of the roof to represent young, pliable tree saplings used to support the roof.

- After checking for understanding by asking students to repeat what to do first, second, and so forth, I passed out the supplies for students to begin making their own longhouses and walked around to assist students who needed help. When their longhouses were finished, each group briefly presented theirs, and then I set them in a safe place to dry.

Assessment Activities, Lesson 1

Some of the informal assessments I used for Lesson 1 were the K-W-L chart for mapping students' prior knowledge from Activity 1.3, the finished poem from Activity 1.4, the brainstorming chart from Activity 1.5, and the pictorial paper from Activity 1.6.

I used the Progress Indicator Chart to record observations I made of students' ability to meet the standards. I also chose two formal means of assessment, which are described in Activities 1.9 and 1.10.

PROCEDURE: ACTIVITY 1.9, STORY WRITING

- Again, I gathered my students around the mural, where we had placed a small table to display the longhouses. I asked the students to look at the mural with the houses and pretend that they were Iroquois living inside the longhouses they had built.

- To give students an opportunity to express their experiences making the longhouses, I asked them to write a story about the process, including their feelings of hardship and success. Two student's stories are shown on pages 109 and 110.

PROCEDURE: ACTIVITY 1.10, PRESENTATION OF STORIES AND LONGHOUSES

Students were evaluated for this lesson based on three main points: their ability to follow the oral and written directions to make the longhouse, the quality of the longhouse itself, and the story written in the previous activity.

- One at a time, students brought their longhouses and stories to the front of the class or a small group, depending on their English proficiency level, to share their story.

Student Story 1

> Ernesto
>
> A last I have finished my longhouse. It boks great! I like it, but it took me a lot of work. Now I can live in a longhouse just like the other indians. A longhouse is hard to do but it's cool. I like longhouses even if their hard to make. My long house is 100 feet long!

- Classmates were allowed to ask questions of the presenter as well as provide positive feedback. I gave an assessment mark based on the presentation criteria shown on page 111.

Some of the students had projects and stories that did not quite fit any of the assessment descriptions and fell between the numbers on the rubric. In these cases, I decided to give an assessment mark that most closely described what the student had accomplished.

Adaptations, Lesson 1

Having a class full of a wide range of English proficiency levels, I always have to make exceptions to activities. The needs of the children help me decide on what I do. Sometimes doing activities in homogeneous groups of language ability works best, whereas at

Student Story 2

Deana

I'm finely done with my longhouse. I'm finely going to rest from all that work. It tolke me a capole of months to do. I like my hard work. The hardest things were choping down the trees, patting them up,

bending them. now I'm going to exsplore it. I thing it is perfikt. My family likes it to well years past bye we are going to move out but first we are going to bild it biger becuse the other family could be biger then mine becuse my family is a small one but I am glad.

Presentation Criteria

1 — Student shows little or no comprehension of steps. Project is untidy and disorganized. Story shows little or no understanding of life in a longhouse.

2 — Student shows some comprehension of the steps involved. The project may or may not be neat. The story shows some understanding of life in a longhouse.

3 — Student shows evidence of following the steps correctly. The project is neat and put together carefully. The story recited shows understanding of life in a longhouse.

other times heterogeneous groups of language ability are best. Sometimes different numbers in the groups works best. The key is determining the students' needs and what works for a particular group of students at a given time. With students learning English at all different stages and at all different paces, I find that the groupings are constantly changing.

For students who are not quite fluent enough to write in English for Activity 1.8, I ask them to recite to the class or a small group what their day would be like as an Iroquois Indian. Sometimes during presentations I find that using different question prompts for students with limited skills allows them to use the English they are confident with. If the students' speaking and writing skills are not proficient enough, asking them to draw a picture of what they would be doing at different stages of the building process is sufficient. I sometimes give the directions of the assignment in the primary language to a particular child. I always keep in mind the content I want to measure and find a way for students to demonstrate to me a successful grasp of the skill or concept, regardless of their English language ability.

Lesson 2 Activities: The Way of Life

KEY VOCABULARY

animal horn	longhouse family
beans	mushrooms
canoe	natural resource
clan family	nuts
corn	spirit
cornhusk doll	snow
cradleboard	snowshoe
fireside family	tree
harvest	turtle shell
hunt	wampum

MATERIALS

Iroquois big book
natural resource index cards
cooperative center materials

three or four longhouse family unit folders
game materials
pasta boxes, round plastic containers
beans, small pasta, paper
journals
Iroquois meal ingredients
copies of process grid

Goal 1, Standard 2 To use English to communicate in social settings: Students will interact in, through, and with spoken and written English for personal expression and enjoyment.

Descriptor

- sharing social and cultural traditions and values

Progress Indicators

- listen to, read, watch, and respond to stories, books, and songs
- express enjoyment while playing a game
- talk about a favorite food or celebration

Goal 2, Standard 3 To use English to achieve academically in all content areas: Students will use appropriate learning strategies to construct and apply academic knowledge.

Descriptors

- applying basic reading comprehension skills such as skimming, scanning, previewing, and reviewing text
- using context to construct meaning
- actively connecting new information to information previously learned
- evaluating one's own success in a completed learning task
- recognizing the need for and seeking assistance appropriately from others (e.g., teachers and parent helpers)
- imitating the behaviors of native English speakers to complete tasks successfully

Progress Indicators

- rehearse and visualize information
- take risks with language
- seek more knowledgeable others with whom to consult to advance understanding

Goal 3, Standard 2 To use English in socially and culturally appropriate ways: Students will use nonverbal communication appropriate to audience, purpose, and setting.

Descriptors

- responding appropriately to nonverbal cues and body language
- demonstrating knowledge of acceptable nonverbal classroom behaviors
- using acceptable tone, volume, stress, and intonation in various social settings
- adjusting behavior in response to nonverbal cues

Progress Indicator

- use appropriate volume of voice in different settings

Activity 2.1: Big Book

Using big books of all types is a good way to focus children on a given topic. The books can be teacher-made, student-made, or purchased. In my search for resources, I did not find a book that presented an opportunity for my ESOL students to gain full background on the Iroquois Indians. So I created one, using an oral tradition text, *The Origin of the Iroquois Nations* (Welker, 1996), shown on page 114.

PROCEDURE

- I read the big book to the students through shared reading.
- Afterward, I paired students at a high level of English proficiency with students at a low level of proficiency. Their job was to write down some things that the book told them about the Iroquois.
- We came back together as a whole class, and the students read their responses aloud while I wrote them on chart paper in the order the students recited them. We then went through all of the responses and put them in the same order as they appeared in the book. Once the responses were put in order, the students copied them in the correct order into their journals.

Activity 2.2: Think-Pair-Share

The purpose of this **think-pair-share** activity was to give students an opportunity to learn about natural resources. In Lesson 1, the students had already discovered how the Iroquois used trees to make their houses. I used this experience to start my discussion and ended the activity by saying to the students, "Look at all the things we can survive on by using natural resources." The students were amazed at all the things they found.

PROCEDURE

- I divided the class into heterogeneous pairs and gave each pair an index card with a picture and the name of a natural resource from the list below.

Iroquois Oral Tradition Text

The Origin of the Iroquois Nations
As told by Glenn Welker (1996)

Long, long ago, in the great past, there were no people on the earth. All of it was covered by deep water. Birds, flying, filled the air, and many huge monsters possessed the waters. One day the birds saw a beautiful woman falling from the sky. Immediately the huge ducks held a council.

"How can we prevent her from falling into the water?" they asked. After some discussion, they decided to spread out their wings and thus break the force of her fall. Each duck spread out its wings until it touched the wings of other ducks. So the beautiful woman reached them safely.

Then the monsters of the deep held a council, to decide how they could protect the beautiful being from the terror of the waters. One after another, the monsters decided that they were not able to protect her, that only Giant Tortoise was big enough to bear her weight. He volunteered, and she was gently placed upon his back. Giant Tortoise magically increased in size and soon became a large island.

After a time, the Celestial Woman gave birth to twin boys. One of them was the Spirit of Good. He made all good things on the earth and caused the corn, the fruits, and the tobacco to grow. The other twin was the Spirit of Evil. He created the weeds and also the worms and the bugs and all the other creatures that do evil to the good animals and birds.

All the time, Giant Tortoise continued to stretch himself. And so the world became larger and larger. Sometimes Giant Tortoise moved himself in such a way as to make the earth quake. After many, many years had passed by, the Sky-Holder, whom Indians called Ta-rhu-hia-wah-ku, decided to create some people. He wanted them to surpass all others in beauty, strength, and bravery. So from the bosom of the island where they had been living on moles, the Sky-Holder brought forth six pairs of people.

The first pair were left near a great river, now called the Mohawk. So they are called the Mohawk Indians. The second pair were told to move their home beside a large stone. Their descendants have been called the Oneidas. Many of them lived on the south side of Oneida Lake and others in the valleys of Oneida Creek. A third pair were left on a high hill and have always been called the Onondagas.

The fourth pair became the parents of the Cayugas, and the fifth pair the parents of the Senecas. Both were placed in some part of what is now known as the State of New York. But the Tuscaroras were taken up the Roanoke River into what is now known as North Carolina. There the Sky-Holder made his home while he taught these people and their descendants many useful arts and crafts.

The Tuscaroras claim that his presence with them made them superior to the other Iroquois nations. But each of the other five will tell you, "Ours was the favoured tribe with whom Sky-Holder made his home while he was on the earth." The Onondagas say, "We have the council fire. That means that we are the chosen people."

As the years passed by, the numerous Iroquois families became scattered over the state, and also in what is now Pennsylvania, the Middle West and southeastern Canada. Some lived in areas where bear was their principal game. So these people were called the Bear Clan. Others lived where beavers were plentiful. So they were called the Beaver Clan. For similar reasons, the Deer, Wolf, Snipe, and Tortoise clans received their names.

Natural Resources

corn	turkey
beans	fish
mushrooms	trees
nuts	tree sap
water	turtle shells
deer	animal horns
bear	snow
duck	

- I asked them to discuss with their partners all the ways they could think of to use this natural resource.

- As a class, we then used a graphic organizer to chart all the resources and what we could use for each. This example is shown below.

Activity 2.3: Cooperative Craft Projects

In this activity, students worked in centers around the classroom, using knowledge gained from Activity 2.2 to create different projects originating from various natural resources. There were many things that students could create at these hands-on centers, based on the targeted natural resource (e.g., cornhusk dolls, clothes, canoes, snowshoes, cradleboards, and wampum). Parent volunteers were essential in making this activity successful.

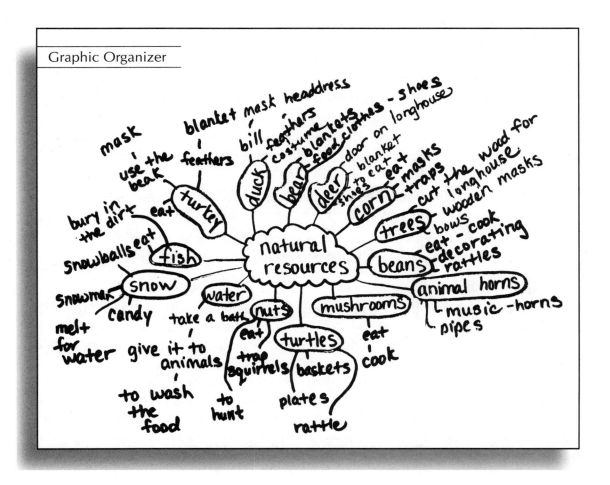

Graphic Organizer

PROCEDURE

- I chose heterogeneous groupings for this activity, but it could also work well with homogeneous groupings. After dividing the students into groups, I assigned them to a craft center.

- When the students were finished at their particular centers, I called the groups to the front of the classroom one at a time to present their crafts. Students reported how they made their objects, what the Indians used them for, and what natural resource they used to make them.

- We placed the crafts on the table next to the mural for all the students to enjoy at their leisure.

Activity 2.4: Longhouse Family Jigsaw

This **expert groups jigsaw** exercise gave the students an opportunity to experience, firsthand, what an Iroquois family unit was like. The Iroquois Indians have three different family units: the fireside family, the longhouse family, and the clan family. The fireside family is a person's immediate family, such as their parents and siblings. The longhouse family, which is the main family unit structure, consists of a mother, father, brother, sister, aunt, uncle, and cousins. The clan family consists of two or more longhouse families. There were only nine clan families that existed among all five Iroquois nations.

After doing much research on the roles of each family member in the longhouse family, I was able to create the eight family jigsaw stories used for this activity. Although the time put into preparing for this activity was lengthy, I felt there was no better way to bring the culture alive for the students than with this jigsaw.

PROCEDURE

- I placed students into longhouse family groups of seven to eight students and gave each group a folder that contained individual pages with descriptions of each family role. The roles are shown in the Iroquois Family Jigsaw Stories on pages 117–118.

- Each student took a page. All students with the same page joined the same expert group to learn about a particular family member in the longhouse family.

- When the students reunited with their longhouse families, they told their other family members what their jobs were each day.

- Finally, as a whole class, we discussed the different roles of each family member. We created a graphic organizer from the information.

Activity 2.5: Cultural Games

To allow students to experience a little about the celebrations behind the culture, I created an Iroquois game fair on the playground by setting up four stations that the students rotated among in heterogeneous groups. This was another activity in which parent volunteers were vital for success.

To create this game fair, I relied on two resources for information about games that linked to this Indian tribe. I used *North American Indians* (Haslam & Parsons, 1995) and *If You Lived With the Iroquois* (Levine, 1998). Based on these resources, I rewrote the games that we played for this activity, as shown on the cultural games chart on page 120.

Mother

In the morning, you get up early to start a fire to cook breakfast for your fireside family—your husband and your children. Before cooking, you braid your hair into one long braid in the back of your head. After the family eats, you and your daughter(s) clean the pots. Then you prepare a stew to cook all day long. That way, your family has something to eat during the day while you are busy. They can serve themselves when they are hungry.

After the food is prepared, you go with your sisters and all the children to work in the fields until noon. The soil is cultivated, seeds are planted, or the harvest is brought in. In the afternoon, you meet with your longhouse family to make clay pots, baskets, cradleboards for carrying babies, or prepare animal skins to make clothes and moccasins.

Father

In the morning, you eat breakfast with your fireside family—your wife and your children. After breakfast, you and the other fathers in your longhouse family go and hunt for game. You mostly catch deer, bear, rabbit, beaver, squirrel, and wild turkey. All the parts to each animal are used. The meat is used for food. The skin is used for clothes and blankets. The bones are used for making tools.

During the day there is some time for fixing things that have broken. At night, you go fishing with the other men in your longhouse family. You take the canoes out to the rivers and lakes. You use lighted torches to attract the fish to the top of the water. Then you catch the fish. At the end of the day you bring all the fish and game home to your family.

Brother

In the morning you eat breakfast with your fireside family. After breakfast you go out into the fields to work with your mother, her sisters, and the children. You call your mother and your aunt "mother."

Afterwards, you spend some time with your mother's brother, your uncle. He teaches you many things. He teaches you how to hunt, fish, make tools, and build longhouses and canoes. He spends a lot of time with you.

You do not know your father very well. You like to watch him do many things. But you cannot be with him until you are much older. You are thankful for your uncle showing you how to do many things.

continued on p. 118

Sister

In the morning, you get up and braid your hair into two braids, one on each side of your head. You then help your mother prepare breakfast for the fireside family. You eat with your family and help your mother clean up the pots. You also help her make a stew.

Then your mother takes you out to the fields with her sisters and the other children. You call your mother and your aunts "mother." You help with taking care of the crops. In the afternoon, mother or your aunts teach you how to make some things. They teach you how to make clothes from animal skins. They also teach you how to make corn husk dolls. You like to play with these dolls with your cousins.

Aunt

In the morning, you braid your hair into one long braid in the back. You make breakfast for your fireside family—your husband and your children. After breakfast, your children help you clean the pots and prepare a big pot of stew. The stew will cook all day so that your family has something to eat during the day when you are too busy to cook.

After the food is prepared you, your sisters, and the children go out into the fields to tend to the crops. The main crops are corn, beans, and squash. In the afternoon, you prepare the animal skins to make clothes and moccasins. All the children in your longhouse family call you "mother."

Uncle

In the morning, you eat breakfast with your fireside family—your wife and your children. After breakfast, you and the rest of the men in your longhouse family go hunting for many different forest animals. You hunt only for animals that are not pregnant with babies.

After you return from hunting you go and find your nephew, your sister's son, and teach him some things. Your job is to teach him how to hunt, fish, make tools, and build longhouses and canoes. You spend a lot of time with the boy. His father is depending on you to teach his son how to become an Iroquois man.

At night, you fish with the other men on the lakes and rivers. You use torches to bring the fish to the surface of the water. You catch many fish and bring them home.

Teenage Son/Daughter

You are old enough to begin learning about things on your own. You walk into the forest to a small hut waiting for you. Your family waits for you to return after many days. You stay in the forest alone for many days. You do not eat or talk to anyone. You stay at this hut until you have a special dream.

Your dream tells you who your guardian spirit will be for the rest of your life. When you have that dream, you are allowed to go home to your longhouse family.

You are now an adult. If you are a man, you now go hunting with the men in the morning, help the young learn how to do things, and fish at night. You will get married soon.

PROCEDURE

- I placed parent volunteers at every station. They taught the students how to play the games.
- Groups of students rotated from one station to the next until all groups had played each game.

Activity 2.6: Musical Instruments

This activity allowed time for making crafts and exploring musical rhythms and beats. The Iroquois made rattles for their dances using turtle shells, animal shells, beans, and other natural resources.

PROCEDURE

- Using cost-effective materials such as toilet paper rolls, pasta boxes, and plastic containers, I showed the students how to make their own rattles.
- I then divided the class in half, and we created a variety of different rhythms and beats.
- We placed the musical instruments on the table in front of the mural.

Activity 2.7: Journal Writing

This writing activity served as an excellent informal assessment of the students' progress in learning the content. It also gave students an opportunity to collect their thoughts and record them in relation to what they were learning.

PROCEDURE

- At the end of each activity in Lesson 2, I asked the students to do **quickwrites** in their journals on what they had learned from studying the Iroquois.
- Students were also free to express any other thoughts they had about the activities.

Activity 2.8: An Authentic Meal

To give students a true sense of the Iroquois way of life, I had parent volunteers help me prepare an Iroquois meal. Many students pretended they were Iroquois Indians while they ate. The children really enjoyed the foods, despite the foreign combinations.

PROCEDURE

- We served corn, turkey, beans, mushrooms, squash, and nuts.
- For dessert, we ate snow food, which is popcorn with maple syrup poured over it. Another enjoyable dessert is snow candy, made by pouring maple syrup over shaved ice or snow.
- After the meal, students shared with the class their favorite foods from the meal.

Assessment Activities, Lesson 2

As informal assessments, I used the graphic organizers we had created as a class in Activities 2.2 and 2.4. Looking at the students' daily journal writings also gave me insight into what they were grasping and not grasping. I used the Progress Indicator Chart to record my observations of students' ability to meet the ESL standards. Two other, more formal assessments were the written summary and jigsaw grid that appear on page 121.

Cultural Games Chart

Stations 1 & 2: Lacrosse

Supplies:
large open field
goal posts
lacrosse stick for each player
small ball

Directions: Divide students into teams of six–eight players. If you have two groups of students at this center, each group can be a team and play for two rotations. This allows one team to demonstrate to the new group how to play the game. Explain to the students how the Iroquois would play against another village, clan, or nation. They would also train for this game and eat special diets. Line up the two teams facing each other as well as their goal post, in the center of the field. The ball is dropped between the two teams and the game begins. The team to get the ball in between the posts the most often is the winner.

Station 3: Peach Pit Game

Supplies:
6 peach pits, blackened on one side
large bowl
large bag of counters

Directions: Have the group sit in a circle around the peach pits in the bowl. Explain to the students that the Iroquois played this game on the last day of the three major festivals: the Green Corn Festival, the Harvest Festival, and the New Year's Festival. Each player picks up the bowl of peach pits and tosses them on the ground. If all the peach pits turn up the same color, the player gets 20 points. If five turn up the same, the player gets 4 points. If four turn up the same color, 2 points are given. If fewer than four are the same, no points are given. Use the counters to keep track of everyone's score and to determine the winner.

Station 4: Racing

Supplies:
2 natural markers

Directions: The racing could be done in a variety of ways. Tell the students the Iroquois had runners to send messages from nation to nation. Sometimes they would have these runners race against each other for fun. I chose to have one-on-one racing for my stations. I found two natural markers for the start and the finish line, such as a tree and rock, and allowed the students to race each other to determine the winner.

Station 5: Post Ball

Supplies:
wooden pole
medium size ball

Directions: Place the wooden pole into the ground some measurable distance away from the students. Divide students into two teams of three. Each team member tries to hit the pole with the ball. Each time the pole is hit, the team gets a point. To make the game more challenging for the students, move the wooden pole further and further away.

PROCEDURE: ACTIVITY 2.9, WRITTEN SUMMARY

For this activity, it was necessary for the students to collect all the information they had learned so far about the Iroquois culture.

- Students looked back in their journals and reread what they had written. I asked them to think about all the things they had learned about the Iroquois.

- After they had collected their thoughts, I asked students to write a summary about what life was like in a typical day as an Iroquois.

- Students who were not proficient enough to write a complete summary drew pictures of Iroquois daily life in sequence. I gave some students passages with blanks to be completed to aid them in their writing. I gave others writing prompts, such as "In the morning, an Iroquois Indian would . . . ."

PROCEDURE: ACTIVITY 2.10, JIGSAW PROCESS GRID

I was able to get a reasonable assessment of the students' progress in this lesson by reviewing their completed family jigsaw process grids. An example of a completed grid is shown below.

- With the students divided into homogeneous groups of four, I gave each group a grid based on the information they had learned about the Iroquois family unit in the jigsaw activity (on p. 116).

Family Jigsaw Process Grid

Family Member	Family Job	Who Lived With
Father	hunt animals fishing make Longhouses	Fireside family Longhouse family
Mother	cook food work in the fields	Fireside family Longhouse family
Brother	learn to hunt and fish work in the fields	"
Sister	help with cooking learn to make clothes	"
Aunt	cook food work in the fields make clothes	"
Uncle	hunt animals make Longhouses teach the sons	"
Teenager	find your spirit become an adult	alone

- After approximately 10 minutes, the class regrouped, and we completed a larger replica of the grid on chart paper.

Lesson 3 Activities: The Iroquois and Us

KEY VOCABULARY

Cayuga	Oneida
Mohawk	Onondaga
nation	Seneca

MATERIALS

observation charts
pocket chart
tagboard strips
large wall map of the United States
copies of map worksheet

Goal 1, Standard 3 To use English to communicate in social settings: Students will use learning strategies to extend their communicative competence.

Descriptors

- exploring alternative ways of saying things
- self-monitoring and self-evaluating language development
- selecting different media to help understand language

Progress Indicators

- test appropriate use of new vocabulary, phrases, and structures
- associate realia or diagrams with written labels to learn vocabulary or construct meaning

---

Goal 2, Standard 1 To use English to achieve academically in all content areas: Students will use English to interact in the classroom.

Descriptors

- following oral and written directions, implicit and explicit
- requesting and providing clarification
- participating in full-class, group, and pair discussions
- asking and answering questions

Progress Indicators

- join in a group response at the appropriate time
- share classroom materials and work successfully with a partner

Goal 3, Standard 1 To use English in socially and culturally appropriate ways: Students will use the appropriate language variety, register, and genre according to audience, purpose, and setting.

Descriptors

- using the appropriate degree of formality with different audiences and settings
- using a variety of writing styles appropriate for different audiences, purposes, and settings

Progress Indicators

- write a letter to an adult or a peer using appropriate language forms
- greet and take leave appropriately in a variety of settings

Activity 3.1: Revisiting Observation and K-W-L Charts From Lesson 1

I used this activity to begin to synthesize what the students had learned since the first activities.

PROCEDURE

- I returned students' observation papers from Activity 1.1 and placed the observation charts on the walls once again. I then asked students to take another look at the charts independently to see if they wanted to add anything they might have overlooked the first time or did not know before about the Iroquois.
- Then I put up the K-W-L chart that we had done in Activity 1.3. We reviewed what we had written in the *K* and *W* columns and then completed the *L* column with information we had learned about the forest.

Activity 3.2: Paragraph Writing

I used this activity to teach grammar, punctuation, spelling, and other writing skills, and also to give students a way to synthesize their thoughts.

PROCEDURE

- For this writing activity, I placed the students into homogeneous groups of three. I gave each group a tagboard strip and asked them to write one sentence to represent what they had learned about the Iroquois. As the groups finished, they placed their sentence strips in a pocket chart.
- As a class, we created a paragraph. We arranged the sentence strips in the best sequence and checked for periods, capital letters, spelling, and so forth. Students copied the paragraph into their journals when we had finished:

  The Iroquois live in the forest. The Iroquois live in longhouses. They eat corn. The Iroquois and six tribes got together. They are very, very strong. The Iroquois have more than one chief. Your uncle teaches the boys to hunt and build. Your mom's sister is also your mom. George Washington learned about freedom from the Iroquois.

Activity 3.3: Chant/Map Activity

By now I felt that students were ready to hear about the other six nations that made up the Iroquois culture. I waited until now because I wanted to be sure the students had had time to build background knowledge about the Iroquois culture and way of life and were ready to understand that there are also subcultures within a single culture.

PROCEDURE

- As a means to introduce the six nations of the Iroquois, I placed six large index cards on the board next to a wall map of the United States. I explained to the students that a nation was made up of many longhouse families put together.

- We used string to mark the boundaries of the area where the Iroquois lived. Then we divided that area into six approximate pieces, one for each nation, and I read a description of each nation.

- Next, we created a chant about the six nations, using the musical instruments we had created in Activity 2.6 for rhythm. We sang the chant three times together.

- Afterward, I gave students their own maps on which to trace the Iroquois territory and to label the six nations.

Activity 3.4: Debate

The debate process gave students an opportunity to role-play a league council meeting in the style of the Iroquois culture.

PROCEDURE

- I first explained to students the process by which the Iroquois ran their council meetings. Problems that arose among the six nations were solved through a league council meeting. All six nations had to be in agreement at the end of the meeting.

- After this, we decided on a classroom problem to solve in a council meeting of our own and ran our own debate using the league council format.

- As their focus for the debate, the students chose to discuss ways to keep their recess playground equipment from being lost.

Activity 3.5: Language Experience Approach

With the Iroquois in mind, we used the **language experience approach** to write what we had learned. This activity provided a way for me to see what new vocabulary, phrases, and concepts students had learned.

PROCEDURE

- We started by brainstorming things we had learned about the Iroquois nations and wrote a group story about the nations.

- After giving the students time to read and reread the story they had created, I typed up the story and gave each student a set of pages to illustrate. They were able to keep their illustrated pages as a minibook.

Activity 3.6: Mini-Talk Show

The purpose of the talk show activity was for students to become aware of how they viewed themselves in relation to other cultures, such as the Iroquois. The topic of our talk show was "The Iroquois and Us." In the end, most students showed empathy for the two students who volunteered to play the role of Iroquois Indians and became very sensitive to the need to be respectful of other cultures. Although not all of my students were comfortable making comments, they all listened and depended on one another to ensure that communication was clear.

PROCEDURE

- I played the host and chose two volunteers to play an Iroquois brother and sister who were sad because they could not understand why people did not like them at their new school.

- I prompted the two volunteers to tell the audience why they felt they had been treated unfairly just because they dressed differently, ate differently, played different games, and so forth.

- Then I took questions and comments from the audience.

Activity 3.7: Letter Writing

The purpose of this activity was to give the students a chance to practice their letter-writing skills and apply them to the content they were learning.

PROCEDURE

- I started this activity using a think-pair-share strategy and asked students to ask one another which nation they would rather belong to and why. We shared responses.

- I then asked students to write letters to the chiefs of the particular nations they wanted to be in, asking for permission to be adopted and stating the reasons they wanted to be adopted. I used writing prompts to help students with limited English proficiency with the writing process.

- We put students' letters together in a class book to be kept in the classroom library.

Assessment Activities, Lesson 3

For assessment, I used many different tools to help me ascertain what my students had learned. I used their observation charts from Activity 3.1, their finished paragraphs from Activity 3.2, their student maps from Activity 3.3, and their minibooks with illustrations from Activity 3.5. I also recorded observations on the Progress Indicator Chart.

Concluding Activity: Partner Skit

To bring closure to the unit, I chose this activity, which allowed students to use the knowledge they had attained and apply it to their lives.

PROCEDURE

- I asked the students to choose a partner to answer this question: "What would you do if an Iroquois Indian came to your school to attend classes?"

- Each pair discussed the question and then shared their answers with the whole group.

- I demonstrated to the class what a skit was and gave the students time to create their own skits based on the topic. The pairs then performed their skits for the whole class.

RESOURCES AND REFERENCES

Children's Nonfiction

Doherty, C., & Doherty, K. (1989). *The Iroquois.* New York: Franklin Watts.
The Iroquois Indians are examined in terms of their history, social and political organizations, religion, customs, and current situations.

Duvall, J. D. (1991). *The Cayuga.* Chicago: Children's Press.
This book describes the history, culture, and changing lifestyle of the Cayuga Indians.

Duvall, J. D. (1991). *The Mohawk.* Chicago: Children's Press.
The history and traditions of the Mohawk tribe as well as the Iroquois nation are the main highlights of this book.

Duvall, J. D. (1991). *The Oneida.* Chicago: Children's Press.
This book describes the history, culture, and changing lifestyle of the Oneida Indians.

Duvall, J. D. (1991). *The Onondaga.* Chicago: Children's Press.
The Onondaga tribe is described in terms of its history, culture, and changing lifestyle.

Duvall, J. D. (1991). *The Seneca.* Chicago: Children's Press.
The history and current situation of the Seneca Indians are examined in this book.

Gravelle, K. (1997). *Growing up where the partridge drums its wings.* Danbury, CT: Franklin Watts.
This book describes in careful detail the daily life of a Mohawk Indian living on the reservation.

Haslam, A., & Parsons, A. (1995). *North American Indians.* New York: Scholastic.
Children are given ideas on arts, crafts, and games that relate to a variety of North American Indian tribes.

Levine, E. (1998). *If you lived with the Iroquois.* New York: Scholastic.
Drawings and text articulately depict the daily life and culture of the Iroquois Indians.

McCall, B. A. (1989). *The Iroquois.* Vero Beach, FL: Rourke.
Photographs and text are used to examine the history, traditional lifestyle, and current situation of the Iroquois Indians.

Norsgaard, E. J. (1990). *Nature's great balancing act: In our own backyard.* New York: Dutton.
This book discusses the interrelationships of creatures and plants in nature.

Shemie, B. (1990). *Houses of bark.* Montreal, Canada: Tundra Books.
Many pictures and diagrams are presented to show the methods and materials Indians used in making houses of wood and bark in the northeastern United States.

Sneve, V. D. H. (1995). *The Iroquois.* New York: Holiday House.
The history and traditions of the Iroquois people are highlighted in this book.

Wolfson, E. (1992). *The Iroquois: People of the Northeast.* Brookfield, CT: Millbrook Press.
The history and culture of the Iroquois nation are presented, from their earliest years to the present day.

Music Resources

Griswold, K. (1994). Chorus of birds, nature's palette. On *Wilderness song* [CD]. Minocqua, WI: NorthWood Press.
A melodic blend of the natural sounds of woodland birds mix with the background harmony of the piano.

O'Connor, T. (1993). *Rainforest magic* [CD]. Nambour, Queensland, Australia: Studio Horizon.
Forest sounds such as birds, babbling brooks, waterfalls, and musical instruments together set a relaxing mood.

Internet Resources

Cochran, M. F. (1997). *Canopy.* National Geographic Society. Retrieved February 15, 2000, from the World Wide Web: http://www.nationalgeographic.com/habitats/86index.html.
> *This interactive Web site highlights the features of the eastern woodlands at different forest ages.*

Fadden, J. K. (1995–1999). *The six nations: Oldest living participatory democracy on earth.* Rat House Reality Press. Retrieved February 15, 2000, from the World Wide Web: http://ratical.com/many_worlds/6nations.
> *This Web site presents resources and information on how the Iroquois nation provided support to the founding fathers of the United States in creating a democratic society.*

Giese, P. (1995, 1996). *Wampum: Treaties, sacred records.* Fond du Lac Tribal and Community College. Retrieved February 15, 2000, from the World Wide Web: http://indy4.fdl.cc.mn.us/~isk/art/beads/wampum.html.
> *This Web site includes a description of wampum: its history, purpose, and significance in the culture.*

Giese, P. (1996). *All native books.* Fond du Lac Tribal and Community College. Retrieved February 15, 2000, from the World Wide Web: http://indy4.fdl.cc.mn.us/~isk/books/all_idx.html.
> *This Native American book index lists entries by subject, age, level, and tribe, and includes individual reviews.*

The Iroquois constitution. (n.d.) The University of Oklahoma Law Center. Retrieved February 15, 2000, from the World Wide Web: http://www.law.ou.edu/hist/iroquois.html.
> *The Iroquois constitution is presented, including the rights of, duties of, and qualifications for the people of the nation.*

Sultzman, L. (n.d.). *Iroquois history.* First Nations. Retrieved February 15, 2000, from the World Wide Web: http://www.dickshovel.com/iro.html.
> *This site provides general history, geography, and demographic information on the six-nation tribe.*

Welker, G. (1996). *The origin of the Iroquois nations.* The Six Nations. Retrieved May 7, 2000, from the World Wide Web: http://www.indigenouspeople.org/natlit/iroqnati.htm.
> *Wonderful selections of stories that are passed down from generation to generation within the Iroquois nation are told.*

Winkler, P. (1996). *Explore the fantastic forest.* National Geographic Society. Retrieved February 15, 2000, from the World Wide Web: http://www.nationalgeographic.com/forest.
> *This is an exciting interactive Web site that teaches students about the forest habitat.*

Teacher Resources

Allen, J., McNeill, E., & Schmidt, V. (1992). *Cultural awareness for children.* Menlo Park, CA: Addison-Wesley.

Ballard, E., Crago-Schneider, S., & Weston-Barajas, S. (1995). *Project GLAD: Guided language acquisition design.* Fountain Valley, CA: Fountain Valley School District. (Available from National Training Center, Project GLAD, 17210 Oat Street, Fountain Valley, CA 92708)

Díaz-Rico, L. T., & Weed, K. Z. (1995). *The crosscultural, language, and academic development handbook.* Needham Heights, MA: Allyn & Bacon.

Ontario/Montclair School District. (1999). *K–12 curriculum guide.* Ontario, CA: Author. (Available from Ontario/Montclair School District, 50 West D Street, Ontario, CA 91762)

Richard-Amato, P. A. (1996). *Making it happen: Interaction in the second language classroom* (2nd ed.). White Plains, NY: Addison-Wesley.

State of California, State Board of Education. (1998). *History/social science content standards Grades K–12* (Prepublication version). Retrieved May 7, 2000, from the World Wide Web: http://www.cde.ca.gov/board/historya.html.

TESOL. (1997). *ESL standards for pre-K–12 students.* Alexandria, VA: Author.

TESOL. (in press). *Scenarios for ESL standards-based assessment.* Alexandria, VA: Author.

UNIT 6
Our Global Community: Different but Alike

BETTY ANSIN SMALLWOOD

Introduction

The children dance around in two circles, one inside the other, as Shawn Martin,[1] the classroom teacher, plays the song "It's a Small World" on the piano.

"When I call 'Stop!,' face the person across from you, take a good look at that person, and tell each other how you are alike and different," Ms. Martin calls out. The music stops, and the children begin talking. Justin, a monolingual English speaker, and Luis, a native Spanish speaker who had been in the United States for about a year, slowly begin to speak.

Justin:	*Well, we're both boys.*
Luis:	*Yeah, and both have brown eyes.*
Justin:	*And we're both wearing cool sneakers.*
Luis:	*Yeah. Right.*
Justin:	*I guess she wants differences, too, huh? Well, I'm taller.*
Karla:	*(leaning over and laughing) Justin has dimples, and Luis doesn't.*
Luis:	*Well, (pointing) me—Venezuela, you—Virginia.*
Justin:	*(quickly) You speak Spanish, and I don't.*

Context

Grade level: Grade 2

English proficiency levels: Mixed, from low intermediate to native speakers

Native languages of students: Spanish, Chinese, Vietnamese, Afghani, and English

Focus of instruction: English language arts

Type of class: Mainstream classroom with inclusion (push-in) ESL model (ESL teacher in classroom for part of the period)

Length of unit: 10–15 hours, spread over 2–3 weeks

The dialogue stops, a bit awkwardly. Observing this, Ms. Martin comes over and asks, "How else are you two alike?" There is still silence.

Luis:	*(shyly) Both play soccer on playground.*
Ms. Martin:	*And you're both good, too. Anything else?*
Karla:	*(jumping in again) They fight sometimes on the playground.*
Justin:	*(softly) Well, I guess that means we're friends.*
Luis:	*Yeah.*

They start punching each other. Ms. Martin starts the music again.

This vignette comes from the Circle Game, an activity in this thematic unit, "Our Global Community: Different but Alike." Its purpose is to build cross-cultural understanding through friendships, starting with children like Justin, Luis, and Karla.

Developing and teaching the unit in different classroom settings with ESOL learners was part of my doctoral dissertation research. This study compared how the material worked in diverse settings: with different teachers, different ages and levels of elementary ESOL learners, and different ESL program models. One of the settings was Shawn Martin's second-grade classroom, with the ESOL students included, or *pushed in*. Although I had developed the material, my role during this pilot testing was as a participant observer and researcher. This presentation of the unit benefits from Shawn's teaching, my observations, our dialogues together, and feedback from others who reviewed the unit plan. At places in the unit, I share how an ESL teacher, Jodi Longhill, adapted this material for her fourth- and fifth-grade beginning-level ESL class, using a pullout model.

There were 16 students present during Shawn's second-grade language arts block, from 9:15 to 11:45 a.m. each morning, when this unit was taught. Five of the students were classified as ESOL, four as intermediate level, and one as an advanced beginner. An ESL teacher, Linda Howard, was assigned to the class for an hour each morning to support these students. In addition to the five students currently in ESL, two others also had learned English as a second language but were then beyond the level of ESL service. That brought the classroom's second language population to nearly half of the students. Three additional students had multicultural backgrounds, and three others had been identified as needing special services other than ESL.

The teacher and students had been together for 8 months when this unit was taught and had operated smoothly as a learning community. The students were familiar with class routines and worked easily in a variety of groupings: whole class, small groups, pairs, and individuals. The teacher was well organized, and the room was filled with attractive samples of student work. It was a warm, comfortable learning environment.

Unit Overview

This unit centers on the universal theme of shared human experiences. These are the things all humans do, but often do differently. In the primary grades, children are still open to accepting differences among people. In fact, they often see no differences, thus making it timely to affirm this value during these years. This unit focuses on concrete personal topics concerning the self and family, such as daily activities. These are age-appropriate and consistent with elementary curriculum topics, especially in social studies, science, and health. In addition, their treatment here expands these traditional elementary school topics to include an international perspective. Through this multicultural lens, the cultures of the ESOL and other minority children are highlighted and validated, thus building their self-esteem.

This unit develops the theme of "alike but different," using as its primary source multicultural children's literature clustered around the topics of daily activities, food, and families. As shown in the unit overview below, it is organized into the following components: introductory activities and games intended to introduce and develop the universal theme; multicultural book presentations (e.g., whole class, small group, and independent reading) to capture the theme through children's stories; reading-writing workshop activities to develop reading and language skills; and culminating activities to bring closure to the theme and unit.

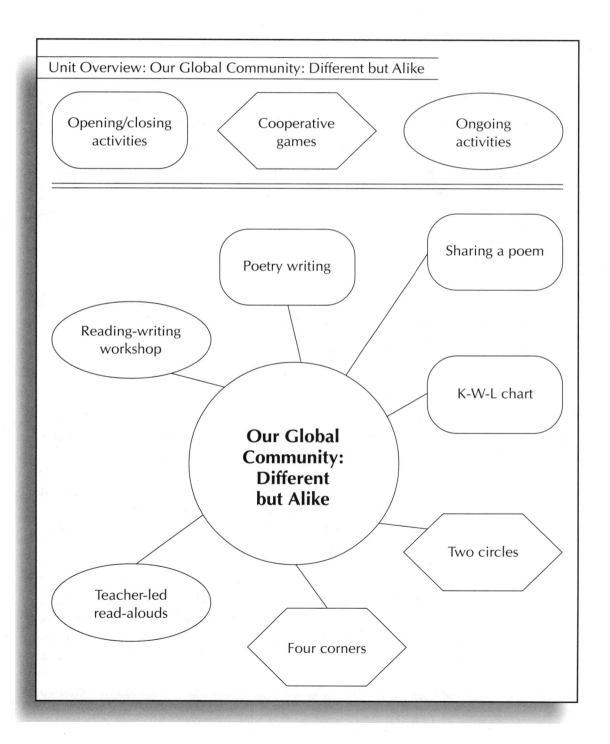

Unit Overview: Our Global Community: Different but Alike

Opening/closing activities

Cooperative games

Ongoing activities

Poetry writing

Sharing a poem

Reading-writing workshop

Our Global Community: Different but Alike

K-W-L chart

Teacher-led read-alouds

Two circles

Four corners

These components are planned to develop the following objectives:

Students will be able to

Language

- use vocabulary related to the unit in an appropriate way
- use the simple present tense to express preferences and describe similarities and differences in daily activities
- identify parts of speech (e.g., verb, noun, adjective)
- use compound sentences with coordinating conjunctions (e.g., *but, and*)
- use *because* clauses to explain reasons

Content

- identify shared daily activities with people around the world (shared human values)
- explain ways in which they are different from, but also similar to, others
- enjoy and value the differences and similarities among people and groups
- relate to differences in a positive, nonjudgmental way
- gain cross-cultural appreciation in the context of a global community

Learning Strategies

- connect new and previous experiences
- compare and contrast
- construct charts, graphs, and webs (graphic organizers)
- learn from others—in pairs and small groups—using cooperative learning activities
- share responses to literature related to the unit theme
- write poems on the theme, using poetic structures (cinquain)

Standards

When I plan a unit, I begin by briefly reviewing the standards, descriptors, and progress indicators in *ESL Standards for Pre-K–12 Students* (TESOL, 1997). I use them initially as background knowledge, as part of gathering resources. As a teacher of many years, I tend to think in terms of practical things, such as books, activities, and children. I have learned that I am mostly a bottom-up kind of planner. I try to match teaching ideas and lessons with students' needs and interests (the bottom part), and then I work upward to connect with unit objectives and curriculum goals and align with standards (the top part). The process is really circular, starting and ending with the standards, with the realities of classroom practice sandwiched in between.

As an experienced ESL teacher, I have an intuitive sense of what ESOL students need. But the standards provide a check of my intuitions and give me the assurance that I have covered all the key areas. With the focus on standardized testing and academic success for all students, most of my lessons concentrate on Goal 2, Standard 2—To use English to achieve academically in all content areas: Students will use English to obtain, process, construct, and provide subject matter information in spoken and written form. Parents, administrators, and even students expect that. But the ESL standards articulate two other goals that are also important: to use English to communicate in social settings

(Goal 1) and to use English in socially and culturally appropriate ways (Goal 3). The ESL standards validate the importance of these goals in a classroom setting and help me justify including activities that help develop them. They also serve as a reality check, in case I have missed any standards within these goals.

Using the standards as an integral part of my planning has two other benefits. First, it communicates to my principal and other district administrators that my program is aligned with current research and practice in the ESL field. Because I have often been the only ESL professional in my building, it is my responsibility to convince the principal of the value of my program. Using the ESL standards is a clear, easy way to do that. Second, the ESL standards help me communicate about my classroom practice with my ESL colleagues in my district and nationally as well. This gives us a shared professional language and vocabulary. Yes, most of us have a district curriculum, and some even have state ESL standards, but now we have a concrete way, beyond the district or even state level, of comparing our lessons, units, and programs. This is an important part of our national professional dialogue as ESL educators, one which is much enhanced by e-mail discussion lists and other electronic communication within our field.

The descriptors and progress indicators related to each standard help me bring the standards to the classroom level and into my lessons. For example, in Goal 2, Standard 1, the descriptors "following oral and written directions" and "expressing likes, dislikes, and needs" (TESOL, 1997, p. 45) clearly identify some of the key language purposes of the Four Corners Game (see Activity 4). Sometimes, however, I have difficulty selecting just one or two standards for an activity, as many can apply. In these cases, I try to focus on key points. "What is really important here?" I ask myself. I find that the process of aligning my units with these ESL standards becomes part of my own professional growth. This is hands-on learning for ESL teachers and teacher educators. And the good news is that it gets easier the more often one does it.

My experience in integrating the standards into my units and helping other teachers do the same has taught me that this can be done before and after the fact. In other words, teachers can build the standards into new units and incorporate them into previously taught but recently revised units. It works both ways.

I use the progress indicators as part of my assessment process. For example, if I have chosen "follow directions to form a group" and "work successfully with a partner" (TESOL, 1997, p. 45) as progress indicators for Goal 2, Standard 1, for the Four Corners Game, then I have concrete language and behaviors to evaluate at the conclusion of the activity. Because the progress indicators are connected to the descriptors, which are aligned with the standard, then by students' accomplishing the progress indicators, I have evidence that they are addressing the standard itself. I formalize this assessment process with the progress indicator chart shown on page 134. The chart allows the teacher to easily evaluate each student's performance by using a 1–5 rating scale for each progress indicator of an activity. It can be completed in short intervals, as time allows, by checking off the observed level of behavior and then indicating the date, with a space for writing comments.

Unit Activities

Activity 1: Sharing a Poem: Introduction to the Unit Theme

The two purposes of this activity were to introduce the theme—that it is acceptable, even positive, to be different—at a hands-on and personal level, and to provide experience with the literary genre of poetry. Because the culminating activity also involved poetry (writing), these two activities served as bookends for the unit. Using the poem as

Progress Indicator Chart

Student's Name: _____ Teacher's Name: _____

Our Global Community: Individual Student Assessment

1 = Never   2 = Occasionally   3 = Sometimes   4 = Often   5 = Always

Activity	Goal and Standard	Progress Indicators (PIs)	Observations					Date and Comments
			1	2	3	4	5	
#1 Sharing a Poem	G 1, Std 1	Volunteers information						
		Describes feelings						
	G 1, Std 3	Tests use of new words						
		Asks about meaning						
		Recites poem aloud						
		Imitates response to question						
#2 KWL Chart	G 2, Std 2	Constructs a chart						
		Records observations						
		Compares and classifies						
	G 2, Std 3	Rehearses information						
		Explains information						
		Consults with others						
#3 Two Circles Game	G 1, Std 2	Responds to game						
		Asks information questions						
		Expresses enjoyment						
	G 2, Std 1	Simplifies directions						
		Incorporates feedback						
		Works with partner						
#4 Four Corners Game	G1, Std 1	Engages attention						
		Volunteers information about self						
		Elicits information						
		Indicates interests and preferences						
	G 2, Std 2	Associates symbols with words						
		Constructs a chart						
		Compares and classifies						
		Gathers and organizes material						
#5 Read-Alouds	G 2, Std 1	Joins in a group response						
		Listens to feedback						
		Asks for clarification						
		Indicates comprehension						
#6 RW Workshop	G 2, Std 2	Names author, title, copyright						
		Identifies main characters						
		Retells and summarizes plot						
		Expresses opinions about book						
	G 2, Std 3	Draws pictures for comprehension						
		Scans to locate information						
		Selects materials for assignments						
		Rephrases, explains, expands						
		Seeks more knowledgeable others						
		Seeks resources in native language						
#6 Poetry Writing	G 3, Std 1	Expresses humor						
		Interacts with an adult						
		Expresses self through a poem						
	G 3, Std 3	Observes and models peers						
		Rehearses ways of speaking						
		Tests use of gestures and language						

a springboard, Shawn introduced the title, theme, and some of the vocabulary for the unit.

Goal 1, Standard 1   To use English to communicate in social settings: Students will use English to participate in social interactions.

Descriptors

- expressing feelings and ideas
- engaging in conversations

Progress Indicators

- volunteer information and respond to questions about self and family
- describe feelings after listening to a poem

Goal 1, Standard 3   To use English to communicate in social settings: Students will use learning strategies to extend their communicative competence.

Descriptors

- testing hypotheses about language
- listening to and imitating how others use language
- focusing attention selectively
- practicing new language
- learning and using language "chunks"
- using the primary language to ask for clarification

Progress Indicators

- test appropriate use of new vocabulary and phrases
- ask someone the meaning of a word
- recite a poem aloud
- imitate a classmate's response to a teacher's question

PROCEDURE

- After copying the poem, which is shown on page 136, onto chart paper, Shawn introduced the author and title: "So What If I'm Different" (Rodriguez, 1994). She asked the students what they thought the poem would be about. Then she asked them to listen first, telling them that later they would have a chance to read it themselves and talk about it. As she read the poem aloud from the chart paper, she pointed to the words.

So What If I'm Different

by Janine Rodriguez (1994)

So what if I'm different,
So what if I'm me,
The me that I really
Inside want to be.

So what if I do
Things that I really like
Like painting purple monsters
Or riding backwards on my bike.

I'm glad that I'm me,
I'm glad that I have
A will to be different
Now that's not so bad.

I'm happy with me,
I'm just a great kid,
I just like to do things
That you never did.

- After the first reading, Shawn and the children talked about things they liked to do and things they never did, two key ideas in the poem. Then they read the poem together, as a class, with Shawn again pointing to the words.

- After the second reading, Shawn asked the students the following questions:

  How does the poet feel about being different? Is it OK, good, or bad?

  How do you feel about being different?

  What are things that make up you?

She needed to probe the students, but after a while, they seemed to understand the poet's positive attitude toward differences and easily agreed with it. They liked talking about themselves and what they liked to do. Most of the discussion was dominated by the native speakers. Linda Howard, the ESL teacher, led a small, parallel discussion with the ESOL students, who were seated near her.

An ESL teacher, in reviewing the unit, suggested a tactile activity with peanuts for opening the unit and as an introduction to the poem. Her idea was to pass out raw peanuts in the shell to the children and let them see that, although the peanuts may look different on the outside, inside they all look and taste the same. This simple metaphor would serve well as a concrete icebreaker and would also provide a hands-on stimulus for sharing and vocabulary building.

- Extension: One of the activities during reading-writing workshop (Activity 6) was for students to copy and illustrate the poem.

- Shawn then wrote the words *Global Community* on the board and asked students what the words meant. Students contributed answers, such as "the whole world" and "people working together." Shawn next wrote the words *Different but Alike* and continued the discussion about differences that had begun with the poem. During these whole-class discussions, Linda again led a smaller discussion with the ESOL students about the meaning of these terms.

Activity 2: K-W-L Chart

The purpose of this activity is to initiate the students' self-evaluation and reflection process about this unit. This involves the students' identifying their prior knowledge, connecting to related experiences, and articulating questions and areas of interest.

PROCEDURE

- Shawn explained to the students that now that they knew a little about the new unit, they were ready to think about how it connected to what they already knew and what they wanted to know. She introduced a large K-W-L chart and asked students to think about the *K* column—what they already knew or had experienced in living in a global community or about differences and similarities among people. One student said that the school was like a global community because the children came from many different countries. Another student said that she learned about this from the book *People* (Spier, 1980). Shawn commented that she would be reading that book to the class, so that was helpful. She then wrote summarized versions of the different contributions in the *K* column. Linda reviewed the assignment with the ESOL students and encouraged them to share their thoughts. Most talked directly to her rather than to the whole group.

> **Goal 2, Standard 2** To use English to achieve academically in all content areas: Students will use English to obtain, process, construct, and provide subject matter information in spoken and written form.

Descriptors

- listening to, speaking, reading, and writing about subject matter
- connecting and explaining information
- comparing and contrasting information
- formulating and asking questions
- retelling information

Progress Indicators

- construct a chart showing data
- record observations
- compare and classify information

Goal 2, Standard 3 To use English to achieve academically in all content areas: Students will use appropriate learning strategies to construct and apply academic knowledge.

Descriptors

- focusing attention selectively
- using context to construct meaning
- taking notes to record important information and aid one's own learning
- actively connecting new information to information previously learned
- imitating the behaviors of native English speakers to complete tasks successfully

Progress Indicators

- rehearse information
- rephrase, explain, revise, and expand oral or written information and experiences to check comprehension
- seek out more knowledgeable others (native and English speakers) with whom to consult to advance understanding

- Shawn then moved to the *W* column—what students wanted to know. One student asked why different groups fight. Another wanted to know why his neighbor Ahmed always covered his head. After recording their ideas on the group chart, she reminded students that they would complete the *L* column at the end of the unit.

- Shawn then distributed individual K-W-L charts and asked students to write at least two or three responses under their *K* and *W* columns, copying the ones from the board or making up their own. Linda worked at a table with the ESOL students to complete their charts. A sample individual K-W-L chart is shown on page 139.

- After the students had completed their individual charts, Shawn gave them an opportunity to share their ideas. She also asked for stories of previous experiences with a global community and getting along with those different from themselves. Some students shared impressions of the dances and costumes at International Day and all the different foods they had

Shawn reported that most of her second graders were not yet ready to do a K-W-L chart as an independent assignment, even though she had introduced the strategy a few months ago. At this point, she said they could develop their own charts after she modeled the process with the whole class and provided sample answers. The children who were at a more advanced level created their own responses, but those needing more support and structure copied selected answers from the group chart.

Our Global Community
How We Are Different, How We Are Alike

K: What I Know

We are a global
community becus
kids come from many
countries.

W: What I Want to Know

Why different groups
fight? Why my neibor
always cover his head?

L: What I Learned

_____

_____

_____

tasted. One student told about men fighting near his apartment. He did not
understand. He said the children played together well.

Activity 3: Two Circles Game

The purpose of this **cooperative learning** activity is to help pairs of students identify
ways they are similar to and different from one another. The follow-up activity allows

the children to write about their experiences in a structured way. This activity integrates the four basic language skills while incorporating movement and music.

Goal 1, Standard 2   To use English to communicate in social settings: Students will interact in, through, and with spoken and written English for personal expression and enjoyment.

Descriptors

- participating in a favorite activity
- sharing social and cultural traditions and values
- expressing personal feelings and ideas

Progress Indicators

- respond appropriately to a game
- ask information questions
- express enjoyment while playing a game

Goal 2, Standard 1   To use English to achieve academically in all content areas: Students will use English to interact in the classroom.

Descriptors

- following oral and written directions
- participating in pair discussions
- asking and answering questions
- negotiating and managing interaction to accomplish tasks

Progress Indicators

- ask a teacher to restate or simplify directions
- listen to and incorporate a peer's feedback
- work successfully with a partner

PROCEDURE

- Shawn told the students that they would be playing a game called "Two Circles," and that it would involve music, moving, and talking. *Music* and *movement* are magic words for 7- and 8-year-olds, so the students were alert and listening.
- She organized them into an inner and outer circle and told them to start moving in opposite directions when the music began and to stop when the music ended. Shawn played the music to "It's a Small World," the children sang along to this familiar tune, and Linda helped the children dance along in their lines.

- Shawn stopped playing the music and called out the directions: "Stop and face the person in the other circle. Now take a good look at each other and talk about ways you are alike and ways you are different." She modeled this interaction with two or three pairs, encouraging the other children to make suggestions.

- She repeated this pattern three more times, as the children were engaged in and were enjoying the game. She added the direction that each time they had to talk with someone new.

- She followed this up with the written component, a worksheet on which students recorded these similarities and differences. She first used an overhead transparency to model how to complete the worksheet, using information students volunteered about their different partners. For example, she wrote *Luis* and *Justin* on the first two lines and then wrote, "Justin is taller than Luis. Luis comes from Venezuela, and Justin comes from Virginia," and "We both have brown eyes and like to play soccer." She reviewed the elements of a sentence, including the initial capital letter and the final period, and reminded students to write full sentences, not phrases.

Jodi Longhill also played the Two Circles game with her beginning ESL class (Grades 4 and 5), but it worked differently for them. With just eight students, there were not enough for two circles, so they just walked around and paired up when the music stopped. Also, Jodi had the students write after each pairing. She felt that they needed the close connection between speaking and writing, even though it reduced the speed and gamelike quality of the experience. She allowed some students with limited formal schooling (e.g., literacy students) to produce just words or phrases rather than complete sentences.

Two Circles Game Worksheet

Name _Luis_
Date _April 25_

Our Global Community
How We Are Different, How We Are Alike

Names	Ways We Are Different	Ways We Are Alike
Justin Luis	I am from Venezuela. Justin is from Virginia.	We both have brown eyes and like to play soccer.

During this explanation, Linda helped the ESOL students by reviewing and then rehearsing this information with them. Shawn then handed out individual worksheets for students to complete during reading-writing workshop (see Activity 6). A sample worksheet is shown on page 141.

- Extension: The language patterns needed for the written component of this activity could be highlighted in a short grammar lesson. For beginning-level ESOL learners, this includes two basic syntactic structures: third-person, present tense agreement, followed by the infinitive (e.g., *Gustavo likes to swim*) and the third person of the verb *to have* (e.g., *Sergio has long hair*). For intermediate- or advanced-level ESOL learners and native speakers, sentence combining could be introduced. For example, *Lubna likes picnics. Rashad likes picnics.* could be combined into *Lubna and Rashad like picnics.* or *Lubna likes picnics, and Rashad does too.*

Activity 4: Four Corners Game

The following day the class played a second cooperative learning game, Four Corners. The purpose of these cooperative activities is to provide experiential learning and personalized, nonthreatening ways for the students to connect with the theme of differences and similarities. In Four Corners, players identify preferences and share with others who make similar choices.

> **Goal 1, Standard 1**   To use English to communicate in social settings: Students will use English to participate in social interactions.
>
> ### Descriptors
> - sharing information
> - expressing feelings and ideas
> - engaging in conversations
>
> ### Progress Indicators
> - engage the listener's attention verbally
> - volunteer information and respond to questions about oneself
> - elicit information and ask clarification questions
> - indicate interests and preferences related to a class project

PROCEDURE

- When Shawn told the students that they were going to be playing another game that day, they cheered. She explained that she would give them four choices, the choices would be placed in the four corners of the room, and the students would have to go to the corner of their choice and tell why that was their favorite.

- As with other activities, Shawn demonstrated the game by walking through all the steps. She asked "What's your favorite thing to do? go to the video arcade? play with friends? go shopping? or go to a movie?" As she read

Goal 2, Standard 2 To use English to achieve academically in all content areas: Students will use English to obtain, process, construct, and provide subject matter information in spoken and written form.

Descriptors

- listening to, speaking, reading, and writing about subject matter
- comparing and contrasting information
- representing information visually and interpreting information presented visually

Progress Indicators

- identify and associate written symbols with words
- construct a chart showing data
- compare and classify preferences within categories
- gather and organize the appropriate material needed to complete a task

each option, which was printed on heavy card stock, she walked to a corner and placed the card in a prominent and visible place. Hands shot up as Shawn read each choice, and she directed the children to go to that corner. She then asked the students to discuss why that was their favorite thing to do and to present their ideas to the other groups.

One student said, "This is a fun game." Another said, "Yes, but it's hard 'cuz I have more than one favorite thing to do." The children were learning, in a social and playful context, that making choices is sometimes hard and requires thinking.

- Shawn continued the game with three other sets of choices, which she had also written in advance on card stock.

    Favorite food: spaghetti, tacos, hamburger, pizza

    Favorite sport: soccer, baseball, football, basketball

    Favorite place to go on vacation: country, mountains, beach, city

- Shawn had finished her cards and was ready to move on to the follow-up writing activity, but the students begged for one more round. She agreed, but asked for their help in making it up. They agreed on *favorite thing to do at home*. The four choices they came up with were *play video games*, *watch television*, *read books*, and *play with friends*. There was, once again, lively discussion about the reasons for their choices. With Shawn's help, the students concluded that many people enjoy many different things, and that is fine too.

- Extension: Numerous ideas for expanding the use of cards came from students as well as teachers during the unit evaluation. One ESL teacher suggested adding pictures to the cards. This would provide visual

Photo of Bar Graph

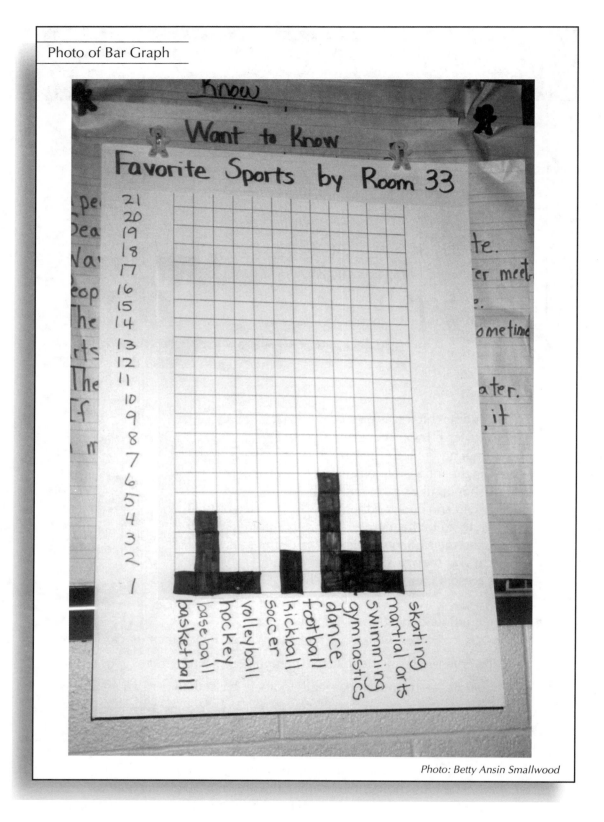

Photo: Betty Ansin Smallwood

reinforcement for emergent readers. One student wanted more cards (choices) and to convert this action game into a card game with rules similar to "Go Fish" (e.g., "Do you have any soccer cards?"). Another student wanted harder cards (i.e., in terms of vocabulary). This would extend the age range of the game. All of these suggestions could be considered by individual teachers and classes.

- Shawn then regathered her class on the rug in front of the blackboard. She explained that now they were going to graph their choices about one favorite category. Many hands were raised and choices offered. *Sports* won, with *famous person* and *video game* tied for second.

- Shawn again modeled the activity for the children, using a question-and-answer format. For example:

Teacher: What will go on the left (pointing)?

Luis: Numbers.

Teacher: Yes, the number of students in our class. Now, what will go along the bottom?

Karla: Sports.

She then wrote the various sports the students suggested. Their final list included 12 choices: basketball, baseball, hockey, volleyball, soccer, kickball, football, dance, gymnastics, swimming, martial arts, and skating.

- Students then voted for their favorite sports, and Shawn recorded the numbers on the chart. As the photograph on page 144 shows, the winner was dance, with baseball second.

- The next day during reading-writing workshop, Shawn asked the students to copy these results onto their own bar graphs. She made copies of the chart on 8½-in.-by-11-in. paper, with the sports written in, and students colored in the number of votes.

The bar graph was Shawn's idea and an excellent addition to the activity. It offered a natural connection between mathematics and language and also included voting, a social studies connection. She limited the students' independent work on this part of the activity, as bar graphs were new. However, just coloring in the squares for the correct sport provided a valuable, concrete task linking reading and math, especially for those students needing extra help in those areas.

Activity 5: Whole-Class Literature Experiences: Teacher-Led Read Alouds

Shawn opened her language arts period most mornings by reading aloud to her whole class a piece of children's literature that was related to the unit theme. For example, on the first day of the unit she read the poem, "So What If I'm Different" (see Activity 1). The purpose of these shared reading experiences was to develop responses to literature and build awareness of the theme.

PROCEDURE

- Shawn gathered the children on the rug and sat facing them next to the easel where she displayed big books. This morning the book was *People* (Spier, 1980). She read the title and author and asked the children to think about what the story might be about, based on the cover. Some of the children who had seen it before said that there were a lot of pictures about how people are different. Shawn confirmed that there were many interesting illustrations and that they would be examining some of them carefully. She encouraged the students to try to remember as much as they could about how people are different because they would be making a

Goal 2, Standard 1 To use English to achieve academically in all content areas: Students will use English to interact in the classroom.

Descriptors

- following oral directions
- requesting and providing clarification
- participating in full-class and small-group discussions
- asking and answering questions
- elaborating and extending other people's ideas and words
- expressing likes and dislikes

Progress Indicators

- join in a group response at the appropriate time
- listen to and incorporate a teacher's or peer's feedback
- ask for clarification
- indicate comprehension of a story read aloud

circle web later. When one child asked what a circle web was, Shawn accepted some guesses, and then said, "Wait and see."

- Shawn pointed to the words as she read aloud and invited the children to read along with her. Some did; some did not. She stopped regularly to check on a word's meaning, to check story comprehension, and to ask children's opinions. The children also interrupted her with questions and comments. The photograph on page 147 shows Shawn conducting the read-aloud.

- This shared reading experience generated much animated two-way interaction and group conversation. Linda carried on many of these side conversations with the ESOL children, quietly reviewing and checking meaning.

- At the completion of the book, Shawn asked for reactions. One student asked, "Can we read that book again?" Another said, "It's more interesting to be different." After some teacher-moderated discussion, the class agreed that it would be boring if everyone were alike. But then one student added that they still liked to do the same things as their friends. They concluded that it is good to be different (your own person) yet share things with others. Shawn affirmed their ideas and said that this was one of the objectives of this unit—to appreciate their similarities and differences.

- Shawn then said, "We're going to do something different, something we've never done before. We're going to draw a web, a circle web, about this book." She drew a circle in the center of the board and wrote *Different but Alike.* Reminding the children of their earlier charts, she asked them to think of ways they were different and alike. With Shawn's guiding

Photo of Read-Aloud, with Shawn Martin

Photo: Betty Ansin Smallwood

questions, the children generated the categories of *food, games, hobbies, pets, jobs,* and *ways of getting to school*. For each category, they suggested examples. Soon, the circle web expanded and spread over the whole blackboard. A copy of a portion of the web is shown on page 148.

- Extension: It would be possible to follow up the circle web class activity with an individual student-made web activity, allowing students to make independent choices. In fact, a model for this was included in the original unit (Smallwood, 1996), but Shawn chose not to use it, as it did not meet her objectives for this activity, which were primarily literature responses and theme development.

- Here are some of the other books that Shawn read aloud to her class on other days:

  This Is the Way We Go to School (Baer, 1990)

Jodi Longhill also read these same books with her beginning-level ESL class, but she spent almost twice as long with each book, expanded them into full lesson plans with more follow-up activities, and usually reread each book two or three times over successive days. The original thematic unit (Smallwood, 1996) included these complete book lesson plans and follow-up activities. Jodi indicated that her students needed the extra time and reinforcement. Shawn felt that as a whole-group activity, half an hour was adequate. I think that each teacher made an appropriate assessment of her students.

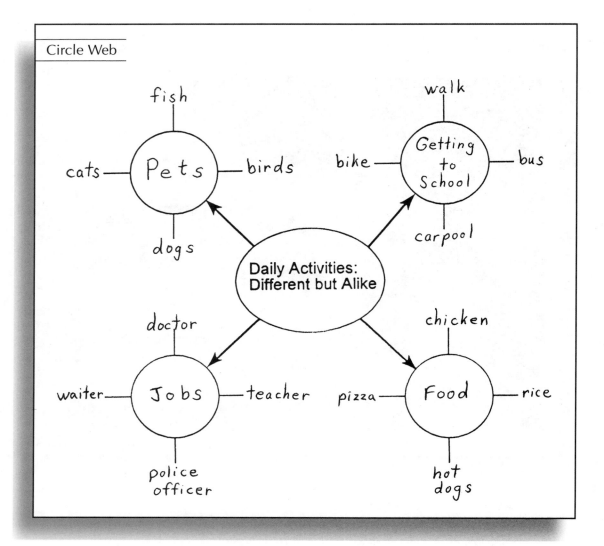

Circle Web

Families Are Different (Pellegrini, 1991; big book edition)

We Are All Alike, We Are All Different (Derman-Sparks, 1991; big book edition)

A Country Far Away (Gray, 1988)

Shawn prominently displayed these and other theme-related books on a bookstand. The students perused them and selected ones they wanted to read independently (see Activity 6, reading-writing workshop, below).

Activity 6: Reading-Writing Workshop

Reading-writing workshop was a regular component of Shawn's language arts block. The purpose of this activity was for the students to develop independent skills in reading and writing. Components included reading groups with skill-building assignments, completion of work initiated during whole-class activities, and independent reading. Shawn integrated this skill time with the thematic unit so that the book content and related work developed a sense of continuity.

Goal 2, Standard 2 To use English to achieve academically in all content areas: Students will use English to obtain, process, construct, and provide subject matter information in spoken and written form.

Descriptors

- reading and writing about subject matter information
- gathering information orally and in writing
- retelling information
- selecting and explaining information
- analyzing, synthesizing, and inferring from information

Progress Indicators

- name the author, title, and copyright of a book
- identify the main characters in a book, their characteristics, and changes
- retell and summarize the sequence of a book's events (plot)
- express opinions (evaluate/analyze) about a book read

Goal 2, Standard 3 To use English to achieve academically in all content areas: Students will use appropriate learning strategies to construct and apply academic knowledge.

Descriptors

- applying basic reading comprehension skills such as skimming, scanning, previewing, and reviewing text
- using context to construct meaning
- recognizing the need for and seeking assistance appropriately from others
- knowing when to use native language resources (human and material) to promote understanding

Progress Indicators

- scan an entry in a book to locate information for an assignment
- select materials from class or school book collection to complete an assignment
- rephrase, explain, revise, and expand written information to check comprehension
- seek more knowledgeable others with whom to consult to advance understanding
- seek out print resources (e.g., dictionaries) in the native language, when needed

PROCEDURE

- Shawn selected three different theme-related books for reading groups, generally matching the complexity of the text with students' reading abilities. She used *Everybody Cooks Rice* (Dooley, 1991) for her most advanced-level readers, *Mufaro's Beautiful Daughters* (Steptoe, 1987) for her intermediate-level readers, and *I Like You* (Beal, 1992) for her ESOL students and others with beginning-level reading proficiency. Linda worked with the ESOL group, while Shawn taught the other two groups, one at a time.

- Both teachers used the strategy of **picture reading** when they first introduced the books. They walked through the books, showing and talking about the pictures. In the process, they provided vocabulary orally for some of the words in the book, asked the students to find some of these words in the texts, and challenged them to predict the stories from the pictures.

- The next day in their groups, the students began reading, in turns. Shawn then assigned them to finish reading the books independently and to complete the book report form, which she explained. (This book report was designed specifically for this unit and included questions such as "How are the characters the same?" and "How are they different?")

- The following day, students talked about the books and shared their ideas and drawings from their reports. One student's book report is shown on page 151.

- Extension: Book making was the extension activity for the ESOL group. In partners, students interviewed each other and then wrote and drew about how they were alike and different. Linda provided them with a model and helped the students compare and contrast themselves with each other (e.g., "I play Mexican stick ball. You play volleyball."). Students wrote and illustrated their own books, which were about six pages long. Much time was needed for the writing process, which included brainstorming, planning, drafting, revising, and illustrating. The students were very proud of their completed books and read them to the class. Two sample pages are shown on page 152.

  Linda found that creating this personalized book based on the patterns of I Like You (Beal, 1992) was too easy for her more advanced intermediate-level ESL group in another second-grade class. She therefore switched the extension activity and had the students answer the book report questions instead. She found that using an easy book with a challenging activity allowed students to focus on the activity rather than on the vocabulary in a harder book. Jodi Longhill also found that this book-making activity worked well with her beginning-level ESL fourth and fifth graders. Their books were slightly longer and had more sophisticated art, despite the students' more limited proficiency in English.

- Some of the time in reading-writing workshop was spent completing individual versions of the graphic organizers that Shawn had introduced and modeled during whole-group time. This included the "Two Circles" worksheet and the bar graph from Activities 2 and 3. Students also copied and illustrated the poem from Activity 1. Shawn encouraged the children to

Completed Book Report

Name: _____   Date: 6\8\00 _____

Our Global Community: How We are Different, How we are Alike

Book Report

Write in full sentences.

1. *Title:* Every body Coors Rice _____

2. *Date Published:*
_____ It was podlisd in 1991. _____

3. *Author:* It was kitin by norah Dooley. _____

4. *Illustrator:* It was Illustrator by peter J.thornton.

5. *Topic: (what is the book about?)*
Its about a little girk that is looking for rear
little brother. She gose to evereones house to se
if near little brother on thih is ther.

6. *How are the characters (people) the same?*
Ever bute has rices in ther house.

_____

7. *How are the characters (people) different?*
Thay all coor Rice with ther own rescene.

_____

8. *What part did you like best and why?*
I like the part when the bleus gave the little
grci a kittin. I like that part becesse I likel kittin

9. *What (new thing) did you learn?*
In this book I leard That people mahe rice
difrinti....To us Its grose rices but to them
mm-mm food.

10. *On the back draw a picture about the book.*

---

help one another on these assignments, although all students were expected to turn in their own work.

- Independent reading on the theme was another regular activity in reading-writing workshop. When the students had completed their group reading book and other work, they could select books from

Teachers can use their own systems for tracking independent reading and vocabulary development. For example, for vocabulary, some teachers like to use large index cards held together with a clip so that young children can easily change the words as they learn them. Shawn used the reading log and vocabulary sheets developed for this unit. She found that they worked adequately for assessment purposes and did not prove too burdensome for the students.

Two Sample Pages

**I like you
You like me.
But let's see…**

I have a dog.

You have a gerbil.

We do things differently!

**I like you
You like me.
But let's see…**

I play a Mexican Stick game.

You play volleyball.

We do things differently!

the thematic display. For each book, there were two follow-up assignments. First, students were asked to complete an entry in their reading log, in which they had to list the title, author, and date completed. Second, they had to identify five new vocabulary words, give a definition for each, write a sentence (which could be taken from the book), and draw a picture. Samples of the reading log and the vocabulary sheets are shown below and on page 154, respectively.

In addition to the semifree reading selections during reading-writing workshop, Shawn also planned time during the week for free reading. This is known in some districts as Sustained Silent Reading (SSR) and in others as Drop Everything and Read (DEAR). During SSR or DEAR, students selected their own books or magazines, without being limited to those related to the unit theme. Also, no reading log or vocabulary cards were required. Interestingly, however, Shawn reported that many students selected books from the theme display during free-reading time.

Reading Log

Name _____

Date _____

Our Global Community
How We Are Different, How We Are Alike

Book Title	Author	Date Completed

Vocabulary Sheet

Name: _____ Date _____

Our Global Community
How We Are Different, How We Are Alike

Directions:
Choose five new words from the book you read. Choose words that are important to you. For each word, write it on the line, give a definition or synonym, and
write a sentence that shows its meaning (you can copy one from the book or
write your own). Also draw a picture that helps you remember the word.

1. Word: _____

   Definition: _____

   Sentence: _____

   Picture:

2. Word: _____

   Definition: _____

   Sentence: _____

   Picture:

Activity 7: Poetry Writing—Cinquains: Culminating Activity

Shawn selected writing cinquains, a formatted type of poetry, as the activity to culminate
the unit. The purpose of a cinquain is to express oneself in poetry while working within
a structured format. Shawn felt that her students needed development in these two areas,
self-expression and structure.

She selected the topic "Me" to bring reflection and closure to the unit. After experiencing, reading, writing, and thinking about similarities and differences in our global
community, she felt it was important to bring the theme back to the personal level. The
objective was for her students to express their own identities and to affirm other students'

identities as well. She also integrated technology, as she planned this activity around her computer lab time, so the students could practice their new word-processing skills by typing their final drafts on the computer.

Goal 3, Standard 1 To use English in socially and culturally appropriate ways: Students will use the appropriate language variety, register, and genre according to audience, purpose, and setting.

Descriptors

- using the appropriate degree of formality with different audiences and settings
- using a variety of writing styles appropriate for different audiences, purposes, and settings
- responding to and using slang appropriately
- responding to and using humor appropriately

Progress Indicators

- express humor through verbal and nonverbal means
- interact with an adult in a formal and informal setting
- demonstrate an understanding of ways to express oneself through a poem

Goal 3, Standard 3 To use English in socially and culturally appropriate ways: Students will use appropriate learning strategies to extend their communicative competence.

Descriptors

- observing and modeling how others speak and behave in a particular situation
- experimenting with variations of language in academic settings
- self-monitoring and self-evaluating language use according to setting and audience
- rehearsing variations for language in different social and academic settings
- deciding when use of slang is appropriate

Progress Indicators

- observe and model language use and behaviors of peers in a poem-presentation setting
- rehearse different ways of speaking when presenting a poem about a classmate
- test appropriate use of newly acquired gestures and language when presenting a poem

PROCEDURE

- Shawn told the class "to put on their thinking caps" because they were going to do something new—write poems called cinquains. They asked "What are those?" and she wrote the word *cinquain* on the board. Together they pronounced it. She explained, "We will write poems about ourselves and then try to guess who each person is, but first let us read this example." She directed them to the chart paper, where she had written the following cinquain.

People

People,

Different, alike,

Playing, eating, fighting,

Hating, hopeful, helpful, happy,

Our world—people.

Shawn mentioned that Betty was the poet. The class read the poem together and talked about how it expressed many of the ideas in the unit.

- She then said, "Let me tell you the form for the poem, so we can begin to write our own." She asked the students to guess and then supplied the type of word, adding the grammatical name, too. The students commented on the set number of words.

One name (noun):	People
Two descriptors (adjectives):	Different, alike
Three action words (verbs):	Playing, eating, fighting
Four feeling words, or emotions:	Hating, hopeful, helpful, happy
One or two nouns, synonyms:	Our world—people

- Shawn then helped the class to write a cinquain together about Linda Howard, the ESL teacher, with her permission. The students did fine with the format and each line, but had some trouble generating feeling words, even after Shawn gave examples.

- Extension: To help the students develop a cognitive awareness of emotions, students can read the dual language book, *Everybody Has Feelings/Todos tenemos sentimientos* (Avery, 1992), which names a number of feelings and links them with photographs. It has the additional advantage of providing these words in both English and Spanish.

- The students went to their desks and began to draft cinquains about themselves. They followed the format, which Shawn had written on the board and also distributed as an individual guide. During this writing time, Linda worked with the

The students concentrated on poem writing for about 30 minutes, which is a long time for 7-year-olds. The room was fairly quiet, with the children working individually, because they understood that the presentation would involve a guessing game and they should not be giving away clues. This added a somewhat secretive element to the activity, which the children seemed to take on as a challenge, as it was a change in the generally collaborative atmosphere of the classroom.

ESOL students as a group and also helped them individually, as needed. Shawn circulated to help the other students, who were working more independently but still had a lot of questions. For example, they regularly asked how to spell words. Shawn replied, "For now, use your best invented spelling."

- After about 30 minutes of writing, Shawn collected the drafts that were finished and moved the class into reading-writing workshop, the next part of their language arts period. She allowed students who needed more time to complete their drafts during workshop time. She told them that she and Ms. Howard looked forward to reading their poems but that she would not share them with any other students.

- The next day, when the class went to the computer lab, Shawn returned their drafts, and the students carefully typed their final versions on the

Student Cinquains

Me
Silly, friendly
Writing, horse-riding, talking
Feeling, loving, thinking, liking
Me

Me
Chinese, quiet
Writing, collecting, swimming
Excited, happy, sad, special
Me

Me
Silly, long-haired
Swimming, typing, dancing
Happy, mad, sad, tired
Me

computers. The children worked from the revisions Shawn had made, which mostly involved corrected spellings. They also illustrated their poems with computer art. At the end of the lab time, Shawn collected the drafts that were finished. A few children took disks back to the class and finished later in the day on the class computer. Three students' cinquains are shown on page 157.

- The next day, when it was time to read the cinquains and guess the authors, Shawn built anticipation by asking, "Are you ready for the big moment—the guessing game?" Heads nodded. Shawn then passed the cinquains out to the students at random. She asked them to read the poems quietly, exchanged several of them because two children had received their own cinquains, and helped a few students practice some words from their poems. Then she accepted volunteers to present the poems and asked the class to guess the poet. Some of the students dramatized the words during their oral readings. Usually the students guessed the right person by the second or third try. Obviously, it got easier to guess correctly as more poems were read. After the students named the person, Shawn asked that person to stand and take a bow. The children clapped, and Shawn allowed some time for the poets to comment about writing, or for the class to add other (nice) things about their classmates. This evolved into a positive class experience, with the students affirming what was special about one another.

  > Cinquain writing turned out to be a productive learning experience for this whole second-grade class, including the ESOL students. The students were cognitively developed enough to reflect on and write about themselves, yet the poem's structured format and limited length (only 11 words) made it manageable for 7-year-olds to create and made them feel successful as poets. For many, this was the first time they had been called poets, and their pride was visible. In addition, the cinquains allowed Shawn to teach grammar in context by naming and practicing specific parts of speech. Some of the students commented that they liked not having to worry about writing correct sentences. As one student said, "I just had to write words. That's easy. This was fun."

- Shawn brought closure to the unit by linking this activity back to the theme of valuing differences and recognizing similarities among our many communities: class, school, neighborhood, and the world.

Assessment

Student progress was assessed for each activity and throughout the unit using a variety of measures.

- Shawn reviewed the students' written products for each activity (e.g., circle game sheet, book reports, cinquains) according to her school's and grade's evaluation criteria. As part of this, she kept records of her students' work, both in process and upon completion. She encouraged the students to select some of their best work from this unit for their portfolios.

- She noted the students' progress on language arts skills (both oral and written) at points throughout the unit, using her district's progress checklist.

- At the end of the unit, she had the students do a self-assessment of what they had learned in the unit by first discussing and then filling in the *L* column on their K-W-L charts.

- At the completion of the unit, Shawn and I reviewed the unit objectives in language, content, and strategies, and how and to what extent they had been achieved. This was part of my closing interview with her, in which we discussed her overall experience with the thematic unit and her students' experiences.

- Also at the end of the unit, Shawn helped the students complete a one-page questionnaire I had developed to elicit their feedback about their learning experience throughout the unit. This involved questions about what parts they liked, what parts they did not like, and what they would change and how. Shawn and Linda also completed this questionnaire. The students commented that teachers did not usually ask them these kinds of questions. Shawn and Linda thought this kind of student feedback would be useful as a regular part of their own assessment process.

- In addition, the progress indicator chart provides an ongoing assessment of how well students are achieving the specific indicators for each standard.

Conclusion

This thematic unit, as presented here, represents about a third of the full unit (Smallwood, 1996). When asked what she would like to change, Shawn replied, "The length of time, because I would like to do this for about a month." The full unit is planned to cover about a month's time for a language arts period or an ESL class. Jodi Longhill, the beginning-level ESL teacher, spent about 3½ weeks teaching the unit. One interesting difference between the two was that Jodi used each of the book lesson plans with her whole group (about eight students), whereas Shawn did full-class book presentations and followed up with just a few activities before moving on to more independent reading-writing workshop activities. Another interesting reflection is that the same material worked with the second-grade mainstream class as well as the fourth- and fifth-grade ESL class. Both teachers found they could adapt the unit plans and materials to fit their own class routines and to meet the needs and levels of their students. A major difference was that the beginning-level ESOL students needed about twice as long as the fluent speakers to grasp similar material.

In the closing interview, Shawn affirmed the underlying concept of the unit:

> I liked looking at cultures around the world and using literature to support them. I have students from all over the world and activities like these build self-esteem as well as enrich all students' knowledge about other cultures . . . . I love the theme and feel it is important.

She added, "It was something all the students could relate to, especially the beginning ESOL students." The students' responses confirmed this. About half of them mentioned learning new ideas related to the theme. One representative comment summarized these ideas: "If you're different, it doesn't matter."

Note

[1]All teachers' names in this unit are real names, used with permission, except Linda Howard, which is a pseudonym.

RESOURCES AND REFERENCES

Children's Literature

Topic: Daily Activities Around the World

Avery, C. E. (1992). *Everybody has feelings/Todos tenemos sentimientos*. Beltsville, MD: Gryphon House.
> *Seventeen emotions are identified with a single word or phrase, in English and Spanish, using photos of culturally diverse children.*

Baer, E. (1990). *This is the way we go to school*. New York: Scholastic.
> *By depicting 23 different ways children around the world go to school, this rhyming book teaches map skills and transportation vocabulary while affirming cultural diversity.*

Beal, K. (1992). *I like you*. Reading, MA: Addison-Wesley.
> *Part of an ESL series, this easy-reading book describes daily activities around the world, implying that these differences are positive.*

Derman-Sparks, L. (1991). *We are all alike—we are all different*. New York: Scholastic.
> *Written and illustrated by the kindergarten class at Cheltenham Elementary, this book shows that although we may be different in appearance, we are all the same in important ways.*

Fox, M. (1997). *Whoever you are*. New York: Harcourt Brace.
> *This simple story affirms a powerful message: On the outside, children may look different all over the world, but on the inside, feelings and emotions are the same.*

Gray, N. (1988). *A country far away*. New York: Orchard.
> *In this book, children in two very different settings—an African village and a U.S. town—enjoy similar daily activities and life experiences.*

Kindersley, B., & Kindersley, A. (1995). *Children just like me*. New York: DK Publishing.
> *Through detailed photos and text, this oversized book captures the story and culture of children around the world, one page and country at a time.*

Lankford, M. D. (1992). *Hopscotch around the world*. New York: Morrow Junior Books.
> *This book describes in pictures and words how the popular childhood game hopscotch is played in 17 countries.*

Rodriguez, J. (1994). So what if I'm different? Unpublished poem.

Singer, M. (1991). *Nine o'clock lullaby*. New York: HarperCollins.
> *Using a clock face for telling time, this book shows people engaged in similar activities that are performed differently around the world.*

Spier, P. (1980). *People*. New York: Doubleday.
> *This oversized and ever popular book captures the physical differences in people's shapes, sizes, skin colors, eyes, noses, faces, hairstyles, and so forth, with exquisite detail.*

Topic: Families

Alike

These books each deal with more than one culture or ethnic group.

Beal, K. (1992). *I love my family*. Reading, MA: Addison-Wesley.
> *Part of an ESL series, this easy-reading book highlights families from different cultures.*

Gordon, G. (1993). *My two worlds*. New York: Clarion Books.
> *Eight-year-old Kirsy Rodriguez tells of her and her family's life in New York City and the Dominican Republic, where her family came from but now visits.*

Kuklin, S. (1992). *How my family lives in America*. New York: Bradbury Press.
> *These stories tell of families from three different ethnic backgrounds: African American, Hispanic American, and Chinese American.*

MacMillan, D., & Freeman, D. (1986). *My best friend Duc Tran: Meeting a Vietnamese American family.* New York: Simon & Schuster.
> *A European American child meets and shares family experiences with a Vietnamese American family. See similar books about Korean American and Hispanic American exchanges, by the same author and publisher.*

Pellegrini, N. (1991). *Families are different.* Jefferson, MO: Scholastic.
> *This book is about a Korean child adopted into an American family.*

DIFFERENT
These are family stories that emphasize individual cultures or ethnic groups.

Cowen-Fletcher, J. (1994). *It takes a village.* New York: Scholastic.
> *A sister tries to watch her little brother during market day in Benin, West Africa, and learns that she has many helpers.*

Garza, C. L. (1996). *In my family/En mi familia.* San Francisco, CA: Children's Book Press.
> *These authentic vignettes capture family life in South Texas. This is the sequel to* Family Pictures *(1989), by the same author and publisher.*

Hudson, W. (1993). *I love my family.* New York: Scholastic.
> *A middle-class, African American family enjoys an extended family reunion.*

Stanek, M. (1989). *I speak English for my mom.* Niles, IL: Albert Whitman.
> *In this family unit of single mother and child, a Hispanic daughter needs to translate into English for her mother.*

Steptoe, J. (1987). *Mufaro's beautiful daughters.* New York: Lothrop, Lee & Shephard.
> *This South African folktale tells of a family that has two beautiful daughters with very different temperaments, each with its own consequence.*

Topic: Food

Cook, D. (1995). *The kid's multicultural cookbook.* Charlotte, VT: Williamson Publishing.
> *Aptly subtitled "food and fun around the world," this teacher resource book contains over 50 fairly easy-to-make foods, with clear recipes and stories from every continent.*

Dooley, N. (1991). *Everybody cooks rice.* Minneapolis, MN: Carolrhoda.
> *By visiting just around her neighborhood, a young girl learns that people from many parts of the world cook, eat, and enjoy rice. Recipes are included. Also see the sequel,* Everybody Bakes Bread *(1996), by the same author and illustrator.*

Gershator, D., & Gershator, P. (1995). *Bread is for eating.* New York: Henry Holt.
> *A Spanish song, "El pan es para comer," inspired this bilingual book, which also weaves in the story of how a seed becomes bread.*

Morris, A. (1989). *Bread, bread, bread.* New York: Lothrop, Lee & Shephard.
> *This book celebrates the many different kinds of bread around the world.*

Shelby, A. (1991). *Potluck.* New York: Orchard.
> *This alphabet book highlights international foods.*

Wing, N. (1996). *Jalapeño bagels.* New York: Atheneum Books.
> *Pablo has to decide what kind of food to bring from his family's bakery to International Day that will reflect his bicultural family—Anglo and Hispanic.*

Teacher Resources

Smallwood, B. A. (1991). *The literature connection: A read-aloud guide for multicultural classrooms.* Reading, MA: Addison-Wesley.

Smallwood, B. A. (1996). *Multicultural children's literature: A cross-cultural, thematic curricular approach for English as a second language learners in grades K–6.* Unpublished doctoral dissertation, George Mason University, Fairfax, VA.

TESOL. (1997). *ESL standards for pre-K–12 students.* Alexandria, VA: Author.

TESOL. (in press). *Scenarios for ESL standards-based assessment.* Alexandria, VA: Author.

Glossary of Techniques

Procedures often vary somewhat from teacher to teacher. The following descriptions represent one widely accepted variant, but implementation may change, depending on the teacher and the context.

Big book: A version of a book in which the print and pictures have been enlarged enough so a group of children can all see the book and follow along as the teacher reads. Big books are usually predictable (i.e., the text is easy to remember because of familiarity, repetitions, or illustrations).

- Place a big book, either teacher-made or commercially printed, on an easel where all children in the group can see it.

- Follow the procedures described under **shared reading** to read the book with the children.

- If you wish, use a pointer or ruler to point to the text as it is being read so the children can more easily follow along.

Book making: An activity in which the whole class, or a group of students, creates a picture book based on a shared book, classroom, or life experience (e.g., visiting a bakery). To make a **big book**, the pages can be enlarged on a photocopier.

- With the class or in small groups, write a story on the blackboard, newsprint, or a word processor based on a shared experience (e.g., using the words from a book read aloud or describing what various staff members do at school). You may wish to write what the students say, as in a **language experience** story.

- Divide the story into parts and instruct students to copy or create a sentence or short paragraph on a page. Ask the students to illustrate their pages.

- With the help of the students, organize the individual pages into a book. Add a cover page with the title and names of the student authors. If you wish, add illustration to the cover.

- Bind the book together. You may want to laminate the pages before binding them together to protect them.

- Display the book prominently in the classroom so students can enjoy reading it. They will take pride in seeing their work displayed. If you wish, allow the students to take the book home to share with their families.

Cooperative learning: Group tasks that involve students working in small, heterogeneous groups of two to six people and require face-to-face interaction, cooperation, and positive interdependence. Cooperative learning activities referred to in this volume include **think-pair-share** and **expert groups jigsaw**.

- If you wish, integrate cooperative learning activities into thematic units to provide structured opportunities for group discussion, language development, and content review.

- Assign different roles and rotate them to ensure full participation. These roles include facilitator, notetaker, reporter, timekeeper, supplier, and checker.

Debriefing: A review process in which the teacher asks students questions about things they have learned before they leave class at the end of the period.

- Ask each student a question about material learned during the ESL class that day.

- If students can answer the question correctly, have them line up.

- If they are unable to answer, give them another question.

Expert groups jigsaw: A **cooperative learning** activity in which different groups of students learn different portions of the content material and then teach what they have learned to others.

- Assign the students to home groups, in which each member of a group has a different portion of the content material to learn.

- Have students from all groups who have been assigned the same topic meet in an expert group. They help each other become experts on their topic.

- Have the students then return to their home groups and teach their portion of the content to the other members of their group.

- If you wish, ask the home groups to complete a worksheet or **graphic organizer** that includes information from each of the experts.

Graphic organizer: A chart, graph, or other visual tool that shows a representation of ideas and the relationships among them. Examples of graphic organizers referred to in this volume include **K-W-L charts, movie frame graphic organizers,** and **Venn diagrams**.

- Use graphic organizers before, during, or after reading or discussion to help students process, understand, and retain information, and to monitor comprehension.

K-W-L chart: A three-column chart designed to set a purpose for learning, access background information, ask questions about the topic, and determine what was learned. In the primary grades, a K-W-L chart is most often completed by the class as a group, with the teacher recording the information on a large chart on the chalkboard or on poster paper. This technique is often used to record what students are learning throughout a unit.

- In the first column of a large chart, write the question "What do we Know?" In the second column, write the question "What do we Want to know?" In the third column, write the question, "What have we Learned?"

- At the beginning of a new unit or topic, help students make suggestions about what they already know about the given topic. Record their statements in the first column of the chart.

- Help students develop questions about what else they would like to know about the topic, and record these in the second column. You may want to discuss ways in which they can find the answers to these questions.

- Periodically throughout the unit, revisit the chart and fill in the third column by recording students' statements about what they have learned.

- At each stage, allow more advanced writers to record their own ideas.

Language experience approach: A strategy in which something the children have experienced and discussed is dictated, recorded by the teacher, and used as a text for reading instruction.

- Choose something the children have experienced together. This could be a playground game, a field trip, a cooking experience, a science experiment, a storybook, closing their eyes and listening, or something else.

- Discuss the shared experience with the students, and decide together what you want to write about it.

- As the students dictate sentences for the language experience story, write them on chart paper.

- Help the students reread the story. Follow-up activities may include reading the story individually or in pairs, copying it, sequencing sentences from it, matching words, and so forth.

- To use the language experience approach with individual children, have the child draw a picture and dictate something about it to you, another adult, or an older student.

Movie frame graphic organizer: A graphic representation of a piece of 8mm film divided into six frames, which is used to sequentially depict information.

- With the students, read a story, study a historical event or the steps in a process, or do a scientific experiment.

- Have the students record the story, historical events, or steps in the process or scientific experiment in the movie frames. Depending on age and language ability, students can draw or write one event in each movie frame.

Performance-based assessment: Evaluation that is based on work that students do in class. The assessment of student performance can be accomplished in a variety of ways. Two common methods are explained below.

- Hold a conference with each student, and choose pieces to be used in assessment. As the student explains to you why a particular piece was chosen, take notes on the student's self-evaluation. Include the student's thoughts, along with your own observations, in the assessment narrative.

- Before a unit of study, design a checklist of expected student behaviors to be mastered by the end of the unit. Periodically, check the student's work and records when the student has met expected behaviors. Keep a log or running narrative of student performance observations.

Picture reading: A prereading strategy that introduces a picture book through its illustrations. This provides an opportunity to introduce key vocabulary, to find some of these words in the text, to hypothesize about the story line, and to use academic language to discuss literature concepts such as setting, plot, characters, and time. Picture reading also builds an appreciation of the important role of art and artists in literature and provides models for the children's own book illustrations.

- Use this strategy after introducing the cover page (title, author, and illustrator) but before reading, whether by you in a read-aloud session or by the students in reading groups.
- With the students, walk through the book, looking at and talking about the pictures.

Portfolio assessment: A collection of student work and teacher observations used to assess student progress.

- Assign folders in which students' work is to be placed. The folders can be color coded to reflect the type of collection (e.g., reading response, creative writing, content writing).
- As work is compiled, place the work (or have the students place it) in the students' folders.
- Assess student performance on given tasks at the end of a unit of study, marking period, or other predetermined period of time.

Quickwrite: A technique used to develop writing fluency, in which students write for a specified period of time without stopping.

- Give students a topic or a question to write about and a short, limited amount of time to write.
- Tell the students that they have to write continually during that time but that they will not be graded on content, grammar, or mechanics.
- When students finish writing, use the quickwrites as a basis for sharing, discussion, or follow-up activities.

Reading-writing workshop: An approach to literacy development that includes a variety of integrated reading and writing activities, usually done independently by students during a set time within the language arts or ESL period. Reading-writing (RW) workshop activities referred to in this volume include **book making**, literature responses, independent reading and reading logs, spelling and word study, and **language experience** stories.

- Introduce assignments during a whole-group time. Have students work at them individually, at their own pace, during RW workshop.
- Have the students keep a folder of their work from RW workshop and show it to you regularly for review and assessment. Pieces from RW workshop can be used as part of **portfolio assessment**.

Shared reading: A strategy in which the teacher reads a text that all the children can see and invites them to join in the reading. It can be used to teach particular reading skills or to introduce new topics.

- Using a **big book** or a chart with print large enough for all the children to see, read a story, poem, chant, or rhyme. While reading, demonstrate various reading strategies, if you wish.

- Have the students join in reading with you as you point to the corresponding words.

- In each reading of the same text, emphasize a different listening focus (e.g., story sequence or rhyming words).

Substitution drill: An oral or written activity substituting words in a sentence. A single-slot substitution drill changes one word; a double-slot substitution drill changes two words. The words changed are usually nouns, adjectives, or verbs.

- Give a sentence pattern, and have the children repeat it (e.g., "The book is big.").

- Model the substitution by giving a cue (either verbal or pictorial), saying the new sentence, and having the children repeat it (e.g., "The book is small.").

- To continue, give a cue but do not model the sentence.

- When the children can easily do one substitution, begin cueing two changes in the same sentence (e.g., "The big book is blue." "The small book is red.").

10/2 lecture: A strategy used to deliver input and give students an opportunity for meaningful processing.

- Give input for 10 minutes. The input can be read from a book or delivered as an oral presentation.

- Allow 2 minutes for students to debrief to others around them about what they have learned from the content of the input.

- Continue this pattern until the end of the teacher input.

Think aloud: A teaching strategy in which the teacher models the thinking processes that might be used during a problem-solving or reading activity. The students then practice or perform it, and discuss the processes they used during the activity.

- Introduce the students to a problem-solving activity. This could be an inference question related to a story, such as a how-, why- or what-could-happen-next-question. It could also be a visual or tactile problem that involves puzzles, mazes, diagrams, or manipulatives.

- Work through the problem or read the text, using natural language to interject thoughts that model the thinking strategies students could use to solve the problem or comprehend the reading text.

- Have the students work through a problem or read a text, and orally report their thinking processes.

Think-pair-share: A **cooperative learning** technique that gives students an opportunity to reflect on a topic, compare their thoughts with a partner's, and then share them with the whole class.

- Give a question or topic, and ask the students to think about it individually.
- Have the students find a partner and compare their thoughts with their partner's.
- Ask each pair to share their responses with the whole class.

Venn diagram: A graphic organizer that is used to help students compare and contrast. It can be used to record similar and different information about two or more stories, characteristics of people or things, literary concepts, and so on.

- Draw two circles on the chalkboard or chart paper, one overlapping the other. Students may also be given individual copies of the graphic.
- Present the topics to be compared and contrasted, and lead a discussion about how the two topics are similar and different.
- In the intersecting part of the circle, write, or have the students write, information about how the two contrasted items are similar.
- On each side of the circle, write, or have the students write, information about how the items are different.

About the Editors and Writers

Carla Frye is a pre-K–5 ESL and resource teacher in Newport News Public Schools (NNPS), Virginia, where she also teaches ESL summer school in a self-contained pre-K–1 class. She has been teaching ESL for 4 years. She is a member of VATESOL and presented on the NNPS ESOL summer school program at a recent annual conference. She holds a master of arts in teaching degree from Norfolk State University and an ESOL endorsement from Christopher Newport University.

Judie Haynes is a K–6 ESL teacher in River Edge Public Schools in northern New Jersey and a master teacher for graduate ESL interns at Fairleigh Dickinson University. She has been teaching ESL for 20 years and has worked with the New Jersey Office of Bilingual Education to develop a cross-content standards model, combining *ESL Standards for Pre-K–12 Students* (TESOL, 1997) and the New Jersey Language Arts Literacy Standards. She is active at the state and local levels of TESOL, as NJTESOL/NJBE newsletter editor and former representative-at-large, and Elementary Education Interest Group chair. For TESOL, she is the chair-elect of the Elementary Education Interest Section and co–content editor of its Web site. In addition, she has authored or coauthored four books on strategies and activities to help mainstream teachers work with newly arrived ESL students, does ESL consulting, and is the content editor of her own ESL Web site. In recognition of her many accomplishments, she was named New Jersey ESL Teacher of the Year and was given the TESOL/Newbury House Award for Excellence in Teaching. She holds a master's in language education from Fairleigh Dickinson University.

Suzanne Irujo, editor of this series, has taught ESL at all grade levels and spent many years teaching methodology and language acquisition courses and supervising ESL student teachers at Boston University. Her BA is in Spanish, her EdM is in bilingual education, and her EdD is in second language acquisition. She is semiretired, dividing her time between consulting on and editing ESL-related projects and enjoying the New Hampshire woods.

Sonia James is an elementary ESL teacher and ESL program consultant in Bowling Green Public Schools, Kentucky. She has focused on ESL students for the past 3 years, although she has worked in education for 12 years. At the local level, she helped design and implement the program her district now uses. At the state level, she helped write the ESL standards portion of the Kentucky Program of Studies. She has also been involved in TESOL at the state and national levels. She is an active board member of KYTESOL and writes for the newsletter, and she was recently elected to a 3-year term as a steering board member of the Elementary Education Interest Section of TESOL. She holds a master's in early childhood education, a kindergarten endorsement, and ESL certification, all from Western Kentucky University.

Carrie Martin is a second- and third-grade classroom teacher in the Ontario/Montclair School District in southern California, where she has been teaching for 5 years. To help the 90% Hispanic population of her school, she has worked to develop ESL standards for her district as well as provide staff training for district teachers working with ESL students. During the summers, she teaches English to high school foreign exchange students from around the world. She is currently working on a master's in integrative studies, emphasizing ESL practices at California State University, San Bernardino.

Judith B. O'Loughlin is an ESL and special education teacher in the Ho-Ho-Kus Public School District in northern New Jersey. She has been an ESL teacher for Grades K–8 and adults for more than 18 years. In addition to classroom teaching, she has worked with the New Jersey Office of Bilingual Education to develop a cross-content standards model, combining the *ESL Standards for Pre-K–12 Students* (TESOL, 1997) and the New Jersey Language Arts Literacy Standards. She is the current president of her affiliate, NJTESOL/NJBE, and past chair of the TESOL Awards Standing Committee. For the Elementary Education Interest Section of TESOL, she has served as a steering board member, is current membership chairperson, and comanager of the electronic discussion list. She holds a master's in ESL/bilingual education from William Patterson University and a postmaster's certificate as a learning disabilities teacher consultant from Montclair State University.

Esther Retish is a K–6 ESL teacher in Iowa City Community School District. She has been an ESL teacher for over 20 years, working mostly with elementary students but also with junior high and adult learners. Before teaching ESL, she was a speech clinician and has found her speech background to be most helpful for working with ESL students. For MIDTESOL, she was the second vice-president and membership chair, and Iowa representative to TESOL. For TESOL, she was chair of the Elementary Education Interest Section and continues as chair of the Nominating and Literacy Committees. She has given numerous presentations at TESOL conventions and has written much curriculum material. She holds a master's in speech pathology from Indiana University and a PhD in international education from the University of Iowa.

Betty Ansin Smallwood, editor of this volume, is the coordinator of school services for ESL and bilingual education at the Center for Applied Linguistics. She taught ESL and EFL for 17 years, mostly at the elementary level, but also in junior high and secondary schools, adult education, and university settings. She has been an ESL teacher educator for 13 years, teaching courses at American University, George Mason University, and University of Alaska Southeast, as well as providing individualized training and evaluation for school districts and state departments throughout the United States. She is the author of *The Literature Connection: A Read-Aloud Guide for Multicultural Classrooms* (Addison-Wesley, 1991) and has written and presented extensively on multicultural children's literature in ESL. For WATESOL, she was on the executive board as membership chair and twice served as chair of the Elementary Interest Group. For TESOL, she was secretary and also chair of the Elementary Education Interest Section (EEIS). In addition, she is comanager of the EEIS electronic discussion list and co–content editor of the Web site. She also chairs the TESOL Task Force on the Reauthorization of the Elementary and Secondary Act, including Title I and VII. She holds a master's in TESOL education from Indiana University and a PhD in ESL and bilingual education from George Mason University.

Users' Guide

Volume and Unit

Grade Levels	Pre-K–2						3–5						6–8						9–12					
	1	2	3	4	5	6	1	2	3	4	5	6	1	2	3	4	5	6	1	2	3	4	5	6
Pre-K	X																							
Kindergarten		X	X																					
Grade 1			X	X																				
Grade 2			X	X	X	X																		
Grade 3			X					X		X	X													
Grade 4							X		X	X														
Grade 5							X					X							X					
Grade 6													X	X		X	X		X					
Grade 7															X		X	X	X					
Grade 8																X	X	X	X					
Grade 9																			X	X	X		X	X
Grade 10																			X	X	X		X	X
Grade 11																			X	X	X	X	X	X
Grade 12																			X	X		X	X	X

Language Proficiency Levels	Pre-K–2						3–5						6–8						9–12					
	1	2	3	4	5	6	1	2	3	4	5	6	1	2	3	4	5	6	1	2	3	4	5	6
Beginning	X	X	X	X	X			X	X				X	X	X		X			X				X
Intermediate	X	X		X	X	X	X	X		X	X	X	X	X	X	X	X	X	X	X	X	X	X	X
Advanced	X	X		X	X		X		X		X	X	X	X		X	X		X					X
Native Speaker	X	X		X	X		X								X									

Program Models	Pre-K–2						3–5						6–8						9–12					
	1	2	3	4	5	6	1	2	3	4	5	6	1	2	3	4	5	6	1	2	3	4	5	6
Pull-out ESL[1]			X	X				X	X	X	X	X	X											
Departmentalized ESL[2]							X								X	X						X	X	
Intensive English[3]																				X				
Sheltered English[4]																X	X			X				X
Inclusion/Push-in ESL[5]		X			X																			
Team Teaching[6]															X						X			
Mainstream Class[7]	X			X			X						X											

Language and Content Areas	Pre-K–2						3–5						6–8						9–12					
	1	2	3	4	5	6	1	2	3	4	5	6	1	2	3	4	5	6	1	2	3	4	5	6
Basic Academic Skills	X	X	X	X																				
Listening and Speaking	X	X	X	X	X	X	X	X	X	X	X	X	X	X	X	X	X	X	X	X	X	X	X	X
Reading		X		X	X	X	X	X	X	X	X	X	X	X		X	X	X	X				X	X
Writing			X	X	X			X	X	X	X	X		X	X	X	X	X	X	X	X	X	X	X
Social Studies		X		X	X	X	X	X	X	X					X				X					X
Science		X		X								X	X	X		X				X				
Mathematics		X		X		X						X		X						X				

Standards	Pre-K–2						3–5						6–8						9–12					
	1	2	3	4	5	6	1	2	3	4	5	6	1	2	3	4	5	6	1	2	3	4	5	6
Goal 1, Standard 1	X	X		X	X	X	X		X		X		X		X		X		X					X
Goal 1, Standard 2	X	X	X		X	X			X				X		X	X			X	X				
Goal 1, Standard 3	X	X		X	X	X	X	X					X			X	X	X	X	X		X		X
Goal 2, Standard 1	X	X	X	X	X	X	X		X	X	X	X	X	X	X	X	X	X	X	X		X	X	X
Goal 2, Standard 2	X	X	X	X	X	X	X	X	X	X	X	X	X	X	X	X	X	X	X	X	X	X	X	X
Goal 2, Standard 3	X		X	X	X	X	X			X	X	X	X	X		X			X	X	X	X	X	X
Goal 3, Standard 1			X	X	X		X			X	X	X	X	X	X				X	X	X			X
Goal 3, Standard 2				X	X						X	X				X	X		X					X
Goal 3, Standard 3		X			X	X						X	X	X					X					

[1] ESOL students spend most of their time in a single classroom and are "pulled out" of that classroom for ESL.

[2] Students rotate from one class to another; the ESL class is one of many regularly scheduled classes at a particular time.

[3] The focus is on fast acquisition of language skills, whether in a pull-out, departmentalized, or self-contained class.

[4] ESOL students are taught English through or in conjunction with another subject, such as science or social studies.

[5] The ESL teacher goes into a mainstream class to work with students; activities may be separately or jointly planned and conducted.

[6] The ESL teacher and content or grade-level teacher are both responsible for the class.

[7] ESOL students are placed in a grade-level classroom with both native and nonnative speakers.

Teaching and Learning Strategies	Pre-K–2						3–5						6–8						9–12					
	1	2	3	4	5	6	1	2	3	4	5	6	1	2	3	4	5	6	1	2	3	4	5	6
Computer Skills		X					X					X	X	X			X	X	X			X		X
Cooperative Learning				X	X					X	X				X	X			X		X			X
Critical Thinking				X					X							X				X				X
Independent Research			X					X				X	X			X	X	X						X
Literature	X	X	X	X		X	X			X										X		X		
Learning Styles	X	X		X	X				X				X	X										
Parent Involvement	X		X		X			X																
Scientific Method			X												X						X			
Use of L1							X		X		X	X	X			X	X	X				X		X

Themes and Topics	Pre-K–2						3–5						6–8						9–12					
	1	2	3	4	5	6	1	2	3	4	5	6	1	2	3	4	5	6	1	2	3	4	5	6
Animals				X																				
Building Community								X																X
Careers		X	X																					
Colonial Life									X							X								
Communities, Helpers	X		X			X	X			X						X								
Environment												X					X							
Exploration														X										
Family	X		X					X															X	
Games										X														
Geography								X		X			X						X					
History									X	X			X			X			X					X
Measurement															X						X			
Multiculturalism		X		X	X		X	X		X	X								X					
Native Americans				X			X																	
Nutrition		X																						
Religions, Values																	X		X					
Self	X				X		X			X													X	
Socialization	X	X								X														
Writing Genres								X								X	X					X	X	

Also Available From TESOL

American Quilt: A Reference Book on American Culture
Irina Zhukova and Maria Lebedko

Common Threads of Practice:
Teaching English to Children Around the World
Katharine Davies Samway and Denise McKeon, Editors

ESL Standards for Pre-K–12 Students
TESOL

Implementing the ESL Standards for Pre-K–12 Students
Through Teacher Education
Marguerite Ann Snow, Editor

New Ways in Teaching English at the Secondary Level
Deborah J. Short, Editor

New Ways in Teaching Young Children
Linda Schinke-Llano and Rebecca Rauff, Editors

New Ways in Using Authentic Materials in the Classroom
Ruth E. Larimer and Leigh Schleicher, Editors

New Ways in Using Communicative Games in Language Teaching
Nikhat Shameem and Makhan Tickoo, Editors

New Ways of Classroom Assessment
James Dean Brown, Editor

Reading and Writing in More Than One Language:
Lessons for Teachers
Elizabeth Franklin, Editor

Teacher Education
Karen E. Johnson, Editor

Teaching in Action: Case Studies From Second Language Classrooms
Jack C. Richards, Editor

Training Others to Use the ESL Standards:
A Professional Developmental Manual
Deborah J. Short, Emily L. Gómez, Nancy Cloud, Anne Katz,
Margo Gottlieb, Margaret Malone

For more information, contact
Teachers of English to Speakers of Other Languages, Inc.
700 South Washington Street, Suite 200
Alexandria, Virginia 22314 USA
Tel 703-836-0774 • Fax 703-836-6447 • publications@tesol.org • http://www.tesol.org/